FINDING YOUR

Ruby Slippers

Transformative Life Lessons from the Therapist's Couch

Lisa Ferentz

———— * ————

Foreword by
Meg Wolitzer

Published by
PESI Publishing & Media
PESI, Inc.
3839 White Ave
Eau Claire, WI 54703

Cover: Amy Rubenzer
Editing: Amy Forsberg
Layout: Bookmasters, Amy Rubenzer, Jennifer Wilson-Gaetz
ISBN: 9781683730422
All Rights Reserved.
Printed in the United States of America

PESI
Publishing
& Media
www.pesipublishing.com

Praise for Finding Your Ruby Slippers

———— ✳ ————

"Lisa Ferentz has written a thoughtful, engaging and practical book that invites readers to look at themselves and their lives without judgment. Her clients are lucky to have her voice dispensing these words, and now the rest of us are, too."

— Meg Wolitzer,
New York Times bestselling author of *The Interestings*

"A magical guide to conquering our fears, phobias and emotional pain! With a warm and affirming tone that conveys, 'I get it!', Lisa Ferentz shares years of accumulated wisdom grounded in research but communicated as if she and the reader were simply sitting side-by-side, deep in conversation"

— Janina Fisher, PhD,
author of *Healing the Fragmented Selves of Trauma Survivors*

"I absolutely love this book! A resource for people wanting to heal into the possibilities embodied in their present-day life, Lisa offers solid information and practices to free oneself from old patterns and behaviors. The questions at the end of each chapter deepen the reader's ability to recognize and experience what has held them back while also pointing them towards the healing that is available and possible in their current life. I recommend this book not only for individuals who seek to heal but also for clinicians who want solid and useful tools they can use with their clients and for their own personal growth."

— Nancy J. Napier, MA, LMFT,
author of *Recreating Your Self, Getting Through the Day,*
and *Sacred Practices for Conscious Living*

"I know Lisa Ferentz to be a very wise and talented therapist so it is not surprising that the wisdom culled from her long career would be simple but profound. You will find in the these pages things that you often say to yourself unconsciously, followed by Lisa's empathic yet liberating perspective on them. Enjoy and heal!"

— Richard Schwartz, PhD,
developer of the Internal Family Systems Model of Psychotherapy

About The Author

———— * ————

Lisa Ferentz, LCSW-C, DAPA, is the president and founder of The Ferentz Institute, which provides continuing education and training to mental health professionals. She is an internationally acclaimed speaker, educator, author, and highly sought after clinical consultant. She has been in solo private practice for over 32 years specializing in trauma, and in 2009 was named the Social Worker of the Year by the Maryland Society for Clinical Social Work. She is the author of "*Treating Self-Destructive Behaviors in Trauma Survivors: A Clinician's Guide*" now in its second edition and "*Letting Go of Self-Destructive Behaviors: A Workbook of Hope and Healing.*" You can follow Lisa's work at www.lisaferentz.com, Facebook, LinkedIn, Twitter and www.psychologytoday.com

Dedication

————— * —————

For Kevin, my soul mate, best friend, and superb editor. Thank you for showing me how to live life full on and for giving me the love, support, guidance, and encouragement that makes it all possible and makes it so much fun. And thank you for reminding me, many many, years ago, that I was wearing the ruby slippers all along.

Table of Contents

—— ∗ ——

Foreword

—— * ——

To read this book is to be in the presence, for 199 pages, of someone with compassion, smarts and insight. I have to say I was not surprised that Lisa Ferentz's book would read like this. I first met her when we were sixteen years old, and despite the fact that at the time she was not yet an acclaimed therapist, speaker, writer or teacher, but instead just another tenth grade theater nut like me, I was aware that she simply knew things. Things that I did not know. In her bedroom at her house on Long Island there was a bunkbed, and we would lie above and below, talking about what was important to us. Often, she would make a casual remark that I would think about for a long time afterward.

So it seemed right when Lisa eventually became a social worker. Though I was no longer an accidental bunkbed guinea pig for her burgeoning, instinctive therapeutic ideas, I watched her grow up and work with dedication on a career that was devoted to helping her clients try to find ways to break patterns that were painful to them, and also to help them be who they told her they wanted to be. It was gratifying to hear that not only were people helped in important ways by my high school friend, but also that she was so dedicated to her work, and did not seem discouraged by the obstinacy of some human traits.

That lack of discouragement, and in fact its opposite—a deep and abiding encouragement—informs this helpful book. Lisa Ferentz comes by it naturally; it's who she is, and it's clearly been enhanced not only by what she's learned over time through education and reading and the general task of living, but also, of course, by what she's seen in her practice. She has described for me the pleasures of seeing people change. For me as a fiction writer, this is good and interesting news. Fiction writers often need to show their characters making the same mistakes again and again. Readers can get frustrated with this (and they sometimes let you know), because they too want to see glimmers of change. Sometimes we give it to them, but often we don't. In a novel, change often comes from somewhere else, someplace that is perhaps outside the realm of emotions.

In therapy, though, at least as I perceive it from talking to Lisa, change frequently happens, though it can be glacially slow or rapid or even hard to see if you aren't paying close enough attention. It can also happen and then unhappen, but that's all right too. What I got from this book is that the process of understanding— the work one does on oneself, and then maybe the accidental dismantling of that work, and then more of the work again—is something best done without judgment or impatience.

Lisa's book advocates for not being hard on ourselves, but for simply paying attention. I sometimes think about the famous quote from Freud in which he wrote that an analyst should listen with "evenly suspended attention." I like this description, because it's neutral, practical, and, in its own way, encouraging. I am certain that Lisa Ferentz listens this way in her practice (I know she used to do that, back when we were sixteen), and in her fine book she encourages her readers to do that as well: to listen to their own selves and take hope from what they find there.

Meg Wolitzer

New York Times bestselling author of *The Interestings*

Acknowledgements

——— ∗ ———

In this book I emphasize the power and importance of self-talk, but what we say to ourselves has its roots in how others have spoken to us throughout our lives. I've had the extraordinary blessing of a large Greek chorus of loving and supportive voices and cheerleaders, both professionally and personally. Many people have lovingly crossed my path and I am grateful to all of you. Forgive me for not mentioning you all by name. I trust you know who you are.

I do need to say a special thank you to my wonderful parents, Sasha and Burt, my siblings, Steven, Beth, and David, and all of my extended family members, including my grandmother, Fay Berklehammer, who watches over me from above. I am forever grateful for the countless ways in which you have encouraged and supported me.

Thank you to my dear friends and colleagues, Sabrina N'Diaye, Denise Tordella, Robyn Brickel, Janina Fisher, Richard Schwartz, Nancy Napier, Susan Kachur, Susan Osofsky, Joan Kristall, Pam Weissman, Trish Mullen, Patricia Papernow, Joy Silberg, Ellen Krieger, Lesa Fichte, Amy Weintraub, Michael Kerman, and Jim Foreman. You inspire me with your wisdom and buoy me with your loving friendship.

Many thanks to all of my incredible Institute faculty, especially Yehuda Bergman and Peggy Kolodny who have been with me from the very beginning. And to all the wonderful Institute participants and graduates, for your loyalty and for helping me to keep growing professionally.

I am eternally grateful to my amazing, creative, and dedicated team: Gerri Baum, Kim Brandwin, and Donna Balinkie. I couldn't do it without you.

Special thanks to the entire PESI team for believing in this book from the very start and for putting me in the more than capable and talented hands of Hillary Jenness, Karsyn Morse, Amy Rubenzer, Amy Forsberg, Jennifer Wilson-Gaetz, Linda Jackson and Claire Zelasko. I am so greatful for your patience and commitment to making this the very best book it could be.

A very special thank you to Meg Wolitzer, my dear friend and gifted writer. No matter how far we've both come in life you will forever be my sweet connection to a long ago time of joyful innocence, hopes, dreams, and wonderful possibilities. "When you've got good friends, you've got a good life."

I also want to thank Marissa Madill and Andrea Thatcher at Smith Publicity for your dedication and creativity in helping us reach and teach as many people as possible.

My gratitude to all of my clients-past and present- for showing me that you really can be afraid and do it anyway.

And as always, extra special thanks to my three magnificent sons, Jacob, Zachary, and Noah for continuing to be the greatest source of pride, joy, and laughter in my life.

Introduction

———— * ————

After working as a therapist for over 30 years two things seem clear:

1. everyone is absolutely unique in their experiences, thoughts, and feelings.
2. there are common, universal truths that apply to all of us.

I know that contradiction seems funny but it's what ultimately inspired me to write this book. There are such a variety of issues, symptoms, and struggles that bring people into treatment, but in the course of my workweek I began to notice the number of times I said the same things to different clients. Whether they were teenagers or adults, men or women, I was spontaneously offering the same advice and the same words of comfort, support, or inspiration. I started to jot down on little pieces of paper the phrases that seemed to make a difference for people. Sometimes they brought about a smile or offered a ray of hope. At other times they seemed to be an important catalyst, opening doors to new insights and profound change.

Although there didn't appear to be anything earth-shattering about these "words of wisdom," they did seem to speak a kind of truth that made sense to people and motivated them to look at themselves and the world through a slightly different and more compassionate lens. As you can imagine, being a therapist and witnessing the growth, healing, and profound changes that thousands of clients have made over the years adds up to an awful lot of phrases on little pieces of paper! I have tried to select the ideas that will be most helpful to you—regardless of where you are in your own life or healing journey.

I have always believed that everything you need to grow, change, or heal lives within you. You have so much wisdom, but if you are like most people you often don't access it or trust in it. As you read through this book my hope is that you find yourself saying, "I knew that!" And then I hope you sit with that knowledge and allow it to be absorbed and integrated more deeply. In doing so you can celebrate the fact that you are so wise, and you can also begin to think about some of these ideas more consciously. This might encourage you to incorporate them more fully or act upon them in a meaningful way.

If you discover that some of these ideas are foreign to you, be patient and kind to yourself. Sometimes your life circumstances and the people who raised you didn't provide you with the kind of experiences or modeling that inspires and allows you to tap into your own wisdom. The good news is it's never too late to embrace new ideas and make them your own!

This is the kind of book that doesn't have to be read from the beginning. Use the table of contents to find phrases that speak to you on any given day. Perhaps it's an idea that's new and your curiosity makes you want to learn more about it. It might be a sentiment that immediately jumps out at you because it's something you already believe or use in your daily life. Go ahead and read that one, as it will strengthen an already existing practice.

You might be drawn toward an idea because it creates some discomfort and gets you to say, "That can't be right!" If you read those passages with an open mind and an open heart you just might broaden your thinking and allow yourself to embrace a new concept. A willingness to do that is really the best definition of personal growth and often leads to the greatest amount of change.

Although each chapter has a different focus and can be applied to a variety of issues in your life, the recurring themes of self-compassion and self-care, learning how to overcome obstacles, feeling empowered in relationships, and being more in the present moment are echoed repeatedly throughout this book.

You will be encouraged to focus less on trying to fix or change other people, dwell less on rehashing the past or worrying about the future, and obsess less about selling yourself short. As you move away from those draining thoughts and behaviors you will start to connect with your own deeper feelings and gain insights that will eventually lead to positive action steps that can improve the quality of your life.

Although I could have written many pages on each one of these topics, I made the conscious choice to be brief and to limit how much detail I devoted to each idea. This is because I wanted each "chapter" to serve as a "jumping off" point for you. Once the ideas are introduced and your juices get flowing, I'm inviting you to access your own inner wisdom and creativity and add to the "discussion" by documenting your experiences and reactions.

Therefore, the end of each little chapter has a few thought-provoking questions and writing prompts that build upon the ideas that have been presented. You're encouraged to add your own thoughts and to think about how the subject matter might apply to your personal relationships or life circumstances. There are no wrong answers. All that matters is how you subjectively respond to the prompts. Give yourself permission to honestly and freely process your reactions. You might come to a new understanding or insight as you allow yourself to identify and address your authentic responses.

Of course you're not limited to the few questions that are offered. If you feel so moved, get your own special journal and delve more deeply into any of the ideas that are presented in this book. Sometimes answers lead to more questions. If you notice this happening, consider it a good sign. It means you're truly accessing your most curious self, and allowing for an even deeper exploration of something that holds meaning for you. Often this yields even greater life-changing insights.

Although your writings are your private work, you may discover that it's powerful and beneficial to share some of it with trusted family or friends. There's value in having compassionate witnesses to your thoughts and feelings. It can be exciting to share your insights with safe, non-judgmental people. If something you've written begins to open memories or concerns that are overwhelming or troubling to you, then getting support and guidance from a mental health professional would be an important act of self-care. Oftentimes journal entries help to jump-start the therapy process, giving you and your therapist a roadmap of meaningful issues to process.

Life continues to happen all around you, offering gifts, lessons, and opportunities for growth, change, gratitude, and connection. Take your time and savor the ideas I've presented throughout this book. Know that you will find meaningful truths that apply to you regardless of your current circumstances. And as you revisit some of the chapters at different times in your life, you may find new meaning or inspiration that comes in handy exactly when you need it most.

Please believe that the more you choose to live by the simple but important life philosophies represented by these ideas, the more likely you are to realize your true potential, experiencing inner peace and contentment. Although the prospect of growth and change can feel a bit daunting, the part of you that is creative and curious gravitates towards ideas and behaviors that promote forward movement, both professionally and personally. So jump in and enjoy the journey!

PART 1

* * * * *

Overcoming Obstacles

Sometimes the first step in letting go of old thoughts and behaviors and finding the courage to accept and try new ones is being able to identify the obstacles that become roadblocks for growth and change. For some people those obstacles are external: a lack of support from loved ones or distractions that keep you too busy to work on yourself. In other cases the roadblocks come from within: a lack of self-confidence, a mentality of helplessness, or feelings of guilt that hold you back.

In this section you'll have the opportunity to start thinking about the potential roadblocks in your life. These obstacles are common for many people and often have their roots in messages and experiences from influential people in their childhood. If you relate to the idea that asking for help or changing your mind is wrong, know that you aren't alone: many families and cultures promote those ideas. If you connect to the behavior of doing something over and over even when it doesn't work you're like millions of other people who do the same thing! Perhaps you make decisions based on how things *used to* be rather than how they really are in the present. These are all potential obstacles you can explore.

Once you understand the possible issues that hold you back you can begin to decide if you want them to keep holding you back. Despite the power they may have had in the past, the good news is you now have the ability to knock down those roadblocks. This clears a new path for you and can set you on your way to genuine growth and the kind of changes that will dramatically improve the quality of your life as well as your self-confidence and your self-esteem.

So with compassion rather than shame allow yourself to be curious about the internal and external factors that have kept you stuck, knowing that this can be the first step in becoming unstuck.

Understanding the Difference Between Then and Now Can Set You Free

There are lots of reasons why so many people often feel afraid to stand up for themselves, use their voice, go out of their comfort zone, take healthy risks, or even feel safe in the world. One complicated reason is because they assume that the negative or futile ways in which those things turned out in the past will be repeated in the present and future. The notion that the disappointments or lack of resources and support from the past will continue to dictate future outcomes is a powerful example of being "frozen in time" and not being able to separate out "then" from "now."

For many people it is painfully real that back "then" they had no power, choice, or control over important matters in their lives. This is partly true just by virtue of the fact that children and even adolescents are dependent, have fewer resources and options, and need to surrender to the demands and decisions of the important adults in their world. Children who are abused or violated have even less control and are even more powerless.

But it's equally true that when you become an adult you get a whole new level of power, control, and choice. You can weigh options, push back, set limits and boundaries, assert yourself, and make decisions about critical arenas of your life. If you aren't grabbing those opportunities and running with them it may be because you mistakenly believe you are still living in "then" rather than "now." The helplessness and dependency of "then," especially for people who have been abused, neglected, or traumatized in other ways, tends to overshadow "now." This can leave you with the false idea that you're still lacking in the ability, resources, safety, power, or choice to take back your life and make it yours. Or if you do make an attempt at change, the outcome will be reminiscent of the past.

In some cases the notion that you're still stuck in the powerlessness of the past might be strongly reinforced by other people who feel determined to keep you down. Perhaps they're threatened by the idea of you operating from your most adult self. In the "now" you have strength and your life is full of possibilities. Making choices from your actual or potential current life circumstances might mean leaving those past relationships behind. Take the time to check out whether relationships with significant others are contributing to your frozen in time mentality. Ask yourself what other people might be gaining by keeping you disempowered by always putting you and your abilities in a past-tense context.

It takes courage to make the distinction between then and now. One way to check out whether or not you are operating from thoughts and feelings that are rooted in the past is to ask yourself "How old do I feel?" when you find it too difficult to assert yourself or impact your own destiny. It might surprise you to recognize that feeling frozen, stuck, helpless, or afraid is often connected to a much younger age. This is a way to explain your "ineffectiveness" or the fear that seems to paralyze you. It wouldn't make sense for a 10-year-old to feel confident about asking for a raise at work, or a 5-year-old to be effectively assertive with a grown-up, or an 8-year-old to complete a task that required an advanced educational degree.

The good news is the very act of asking "How old do I feel?" can be the first reality check towards getting out of "then" and firmly back into "now." Once you have the awareness that you are thinking and feeling from a younger place, you can gently challenge the notion of your powerlessness and remind yourself of your *current* age, situation in life, resources, support systems, and abilities. You can also remind yourself that even if your attempt falls short it won't have the same devastating impact that it did in the past. This can help reduce the sense of riskiness and give you the courage you need to try.

The things you're currently trying to achieve can only be accomplished when all of the available adult resources and supports are accessed. Pay attention to your posture and physical stance. Notice how you dress. Even those things can be representative of 'then" versus "now." You can also access your most adult self when you re-connect with the mindset that goes with a capable, independent adult. An important life lesson is not to place the outcomes of "then" on your current expectations and assumptions. Recognize that in the "now" your thoughts, feelings, and behaviors are your choice. In the "now" your life is full of possibilities. And the current choices, power, and control that exist in your life can set you free!

Questions For Continued Growth

— * —

1. Describe a negative past event that you assume will be repeated in the future.

_____

_____

_____

_____

_____

_____

_____

_____

2. What impact does it have on you to make that assumption?

_____

_____

_____

_____

_____

_____

_____

_____

3. Identify someone who contributes to keeping you stuck in "then" and what they might gain from promoting that idea.

_____

_____

_____

_____

_____

_____

_____

_____

4. Identify two ways in which "then" is different from "now."

_____

_____

_____

_____

_____

_____

_____

_____

_____

5. Identify two options or choices you have "now" that you didn't have "then."

_____

_____

_____

_____

_____

_____

_____

_____

6. What impact does it have on you when you make those distinctions?

_____

_____

_____

_____

_____

_____

_____

_____

There's No Such Thing as You Made Your Bed Now Lie in It

Many people who were raised in abusive, neglectful, or dysfunctional families were taught this life philosophy in childhood. It's a message that's typically passed from one generation to the next. Oftentimes the people who model this idea were victimized in some way and went through life powerless to change their difficult situation. Once this got normalized for them, they assumed your life would play out in a similar fashion. They unconsciously contributed to your potential helplessness by teaching you that you would have limited choices in life and once you made those choices, you would be stuck with them.

This mindset also supports the idea that changing "beds" is irresponsible, selfish, or immature. It's designed to make you feel guilt and shame. It's often fueled by cultural or societal norms that look down upon challenging, deviating from, or re-writing well-established spoken or unspoken rules about our obligations to family, work, or other relationships.

Limiting your options is a powerful and destructive mantra to live your life by as it discounts many of the basic rights you possess as a human being. Those rights include the ability to continually re-evaluate your choices in life, to reassess your decisions, to change your mind and your course of action whenever circumstances dictate. You may have made certain important decisions at a time in your life when you were influenced by a lack of experience or wisdom, pressure from other people, a lack of emotional maturity or positive self-esteem, or the unconscious re-playing of what was modeled and normalized for you in childhood.

One of the best and most exciting things about you is that you're forever evolving. The personal, academic, and professional decisions that met your needs 5, 10, or 20 years ago may be completely irrelevant to your life today. Perhaps your eyes have been opened in ways they never were before. Maybe you tapped into a creative, curious, or adventurous part of yourself that wasn't as available in the past, and that new part has very different needs and desires. Maybe the choices you've made have served you well and you've simply outgrown them now.

It makes no sense to say that you should ever be stuck with a choice that worked in the past but is no longer useful, relevant, productive, or safe in the present. You have the right to leave that "bed" and discover a new one that truly reflects who you are and what you currently need and desire. This is especially important when you made those prior decisions under pressure or stress. Or you discover that you've actually been lying on a harmful "bed of nails."

Anyone who insists that you have to forever stay with your original choices is asking you to remain frozen in time. They may push the idea because it meets their own personal agenda or needs, without considering the impact that it's having on you and your life. You may have noticed that other people can be quick to weigh in, without you even asking for their opinion. Yet they'll give you advice about what they think is in your best interests. They make sweeping statements and judgments about your life even when they don't know the whole story. They're often out of touch with your current needs and feelings or the toll your choices are taking on your physical, emotional, spiritual, and mental health.

Even when the "you made your bed now lie in it" message comes from well-meaning people in your life, they may be indirectly contributing to your ongoing unhappiness or lack of safety. Consider the strong possibility that they're taking away from you your right to grow and change, and your right to acknowledge and honor a new internal voice that isn't afraid to try something new or improve the quality of your life.

People who reinforce the idea that you only have limited options and don't have the right to change your mind may be projecting onto you the life that they, unfortunately, were forced to live. Although you can respect their limited perspective and don't need to challenge the fact that *they* have spent their life "frozen in time," that certainly does not have to be your fate.

Besides, how can you possibly know as a teenager or young adult what you will want to be doing 30 or 40 years later? A true sign of an ever-evolving person is one who can look back and identify many "beds" they got to try out, live in for a time, and then moved on. Hopefully you can see that this is the healthiest and most productive way to live your life.

Questions For Continued Growth

————— * —————

1. Who are the people in your life who promote the idea that "you made your bed now lie in it?"

   _____

   _____

   _____

   _____

   _____

   _____

   _____

   _____

   _____

2. What impact has it had on their lives to operate from that mindset?

   _____

   _____

   _____

   _____

   _____

   _____

   _____

   _____

   _____

3. What impact has it had on your life to operate from
    that mindset?

    _____

    _____

    _____

    _____

    _____

    _____

    _____

    _____

    _____

4. What shift or changes would occur in your life if you let go of
    that philosophy?

    _____

    _____

    _____

    _____

    _____

    _____

    _____

    _____

    _____

5. Describe one "bed" in your life that you've been lying in too long.

_____

_____

_____

_____

_____

_____

_____

_____

6. Name one baby step you could take to get out of that bed.

_____

_____

_____

_____

_____

_____

_____

_____

Asking for Help is a Sign of Strength, Not Weakness

Like many people, you may have grown up with the message that the real indicator of personal strength is the ability to handle all of your feelings and whatever happens in life—and to handle it alone. Turning to other people and leaning on them for advice, comfort, or a helping hand is somehow seen as a sign of weakness or even a failure. Even if the emotion is overwhelming, or the challenge you're faced with is brand new to you or is a totally unexpected curveball, you're somehow supposed to know what to do and how to manage it on your own.

The truth is, when you're faced with feelings or experiences that are challenging, frightening, or hard to navigate, reaching out for support is a genuine sign of strength. It means you care enough about yourself to increase the odds that things will work out and you'll get the help you need to successfully meet the challenge head on. Refusing to turn to others for input or guidance is like refusing a lifejacket when the tide unexpectedly changes and you suddenly find yourself adrift in 50 feet of water.

If you do struggle with the idea of asking for help it's useful to understand where your reluctance comes from. Is it an unfair burden you put on yourself that gets fueled by the notion that you should "just know" what to do in any given situation? If that's the case, consider the idea that you couldn't possibly "just know" how to speak Greek if someone from Greece started to talk with you, or "just know" how to land an airplane if you were suddenly sitting in the pilot's seat. The arrival of these unforeseen situations doesn't automatically and magically make you capable of knowing what to do or how to respond. This is particularly true if no one ever taught you what to do and you never had the chance to practice.

The same holds true for many of life's stressors and challenges. If you've never confronted them before how could you know how to respond? And even if the crisis or conflict is a familiar, recurring one, it doesn't mean you'll always know what to do as each new situation arises. Circumstances change and a strategy that worked in the past might be ineffective now. Or perhaps the event occurred in a different context and there were resources for support that no longer exist. In those cases allowing yourself to seek outside guidance is critically important.

If you have spent much of your life avoiding feelings that are scary or overwhelming and then do an about-face and find the strength to address them, or slow down enough that they begin to resurface on their own, you can't be expected to "just know" how to cope with those emotions by yourself. It makes sense that you would benefit from guidance as you attempt to navigate those feelings in healthy and productive ways.

Another possible reason why you might falsely believe that asking for help is a sign of weakness relates to a matter of pride. If you don't handle it all by yourself then somehow the end result doesn't count. But again, identifying and using other resources is a part of the success! It speaks to your ingenuity and humility.

And do you really want the issue of pride to outweigh getting the outcome you're seeking?

Consider the possibility that your grandparents, parents, or siblings modeled the idea that you have to handle life's challenges alone. Maybe they had no choice and did handle things alone, with varying degrees of success. Just because they either had to do it that way, or refused support when it was offered, doesn't mean that you have to follow in their footsteps. And it doesn't mean that you have to buy into the idea that it somehow made them braver or stronger to do it alone. Most often handling difficulties alone is lonely, incredibly stressful, and overwhelming. It's not a badge of courage. You're far more likely to make bad decisions when there's no one to run things by, and it's really hard to see the forest for the trees when you're in it alone.

Another powerful possibility is once upon a time you did reach out for help and support and came up empty-handed. Perhaps your requests for help were minimized, ridiculed, or ignored. If that's the case you may have adopted the idea of not asking for help as a way to protect yourself from additional pain or rejection. It might feel emotionally safer to just manage on your own and not let others ever know when you're struggling or overwhelmed. If you relate to this, know that your attempt to protect yourself is understandable. And yet you're still doing yourself a disservice by assuming the reactions you got in the past when you reached out will be the same responses you get in the present and the future.

However, it's important to be selective about the people you turn to for assistance when you do find the courage to ask for support. If you keep extending your hand to the same person and, rather than lovingly holding it, they slap it or push it away, then it does become necessary to stop reaching out to that particular person. But remember, the life lesson is to choose wisely, not to stop reaching out! It only makes sense to reach out to people who also believe that getting support and guidance is a sign of strength. They will be honored that you asked them and more than willing to help you succeed.

Questions For Continued Growth

———— * ————

1. While you were growing up what messages did you get about asking for help?

\
\
\
\
\
\
\
\

2. What do you imagine would happen if you did reach out for support when you needed it?

\
\
\
\
\
\
\
\

3. What are the situations in your life that would benefit from
   outside help and support?

   _____

   _____

   _____

   _____

   _____

   _____

   _____

   _____

4. Who are the people in your life who would be safe to reach out to
   for assistance?

   _____

   _____

   _____

   _____

   _____

   _____

   _____

   _____

5. What resources are available to you if you did reach out for support or guidance?

_____

_____

_____

_____

_____

_____

_____

_____

6. List some of the reasons why asking for help can be a sign of your personal strength.

_____

_____

_____

_____

_____

_____

_____

_____

Banging Your Head Against a Brick Wall Never Moves the Wall—It Just Gives You a Concussion

Sounds logical, right? And yet you've probably spent a lot of precious time trying to move that wall! As you go through life it's important to understand what is and is not in your power to control and change. A hallmark of continued emotional growth is the ability to let go of what you can't change. Attempting to alter something that you can't becomes a huge waste of energy that could be used in much more constructive ways.

The life lesson in this chapter emphasizes how damaging it can be to your mind, body, and spirit when you keep running up against the different "brick walls' in your life, along with the realization that this behavior hurts you much more than it ever hurts the "wall." Think about the "brick walls" in your life. They can be represented in many different ways. It might be the person who is stubborn, insensitive, or rigid, refusing to acknowledge your feelings, needs, or your point of view. In many cases it can feel like they have built a brick wall around their hearts or minds. This can pertain to your partner, your boss, a family member, or a friend.

You continually run into them with full force, hoping to shift their position, get them to "see the light," to become more flexible, accommodating, validating, cooperative, or caring. After all, you deserve that! And yet it doesn't happen. They remain immobile, unfeeling, even lacking in empathy, and after repeatedly banging your head against that brick wall *you* wind up with the "concussion." You're the one who gets hurt and they're fine. That's worth noticing.

When you understand that your efforts yield nothing but personal hurt or harm you have reached an important crossroad. One path leads to redoubling your efforts, or stewing in frustration and bitterness about the other person's rigidity or passivity. Another path can lead you to a place of courage, where you take the emphasis off the other person and begin to think about what *you* can do differently. Sometimes it means walking around the wall. Sometimes it means walking away from the wall.

Does the metaphor of the brick wall relate to other things in your life? It often applies if you're working in a toxic or dysfunctional workplace. Have you repeatedly tried to advocate for changes in policy, working conditions, the treatment of employees, salaries, and other benefits? Often when you're the only voice of reason, the only one to find the courage to identify work-related problems, or attempt to go up against a well-established and accepted workplace culture, it can leave you feeling alienated or excluded. It can even threaten your job security or put a glass ceiling on professional advancement.

Brick walls can also manifest in other situations or life circumstances that you don't like and try desperately to fight against or change. This can relate to the hand you've been dealt regarding an important life issue such as your health or mental well-being. Even in these situations it's essential to understand and accept when something is immoveable and then redirect your energy and focus to attend to and influence the things that will yield an actual response and different outcome for you.

Although you should always be applauded for your courage in attempting to "take on" the wall, you also have the right to reconsider your options if there are no indications that the brick wall will move and you will be the one winding up with the concussion. Again, giving yourself permission to leave a toxic or completely inflexible job, work environment, or relationship is never a failure and always an act of self-care.

Running into a brick wall or attacking it with a chisel are proactive and obvious attempts to move it, but it's possible that the way in which you do it is more subtle or passive. You might be infinitely patient, giving the brick wall a never-ending supply of "one more chances." You might try to flatter the "wall," trying to manipulate or trick it into "moving." Ultimately the outcome is still the same. It's not going anywhere and you're the one who is frustrated or suffering.

Sometimes there's an ongoing investment in moving the wall and a willingness to suffer the consequences of a "concussion" because there's anxiety or fear about what will happen if the wall doesn't budge. It's worth exploring what your possible fears are about this, as they might be unrealistic, based on something from your past, or less troubling than you're imagining.

There's no question that when you were a child an immoveable wall was a genuinely scary thing. But you might be projecting those same childhood fears onto your present, adult situation, and in doing so you're overestimating the consequences and underestimating your ability to cope with them. As an empowered adult you can walk away from a lot of "walls." And when you do, you're truly engaging in an act of self-care or even self-preservation. Your real obligation is to protect yourself. The "wall" will still be standing. You need to be too!

Questions For Continued Growth

———— * ————

1. What are some of the "brick walls" you've tried to move in your life?

_____

_____

_____

_____

_____

_____

_____

2. How have you tried to move them?

_____

_____

_____

_____

_____

_____

_____

_____

3. What's been the end result for you?

_____

_____

_____

_____

_____

_____

_____

_____

4. What would it take for you to decide to stop banging into those walls?

_____

_____

_____

_____

_____

_____

_____

_____

_____

5. Once you decided to stop running into the walls how could you handle them differently?

_____

_____

_____

_____

_____

_____

_____

_____

_____

6. List three ways in which your energy could be better spent if you no longer used it to run into walls.

_____

_____

_____

_____

_____

_____

_____

_____

If Something Doesn't Work, Don't Do it More, and Harder

This is one of the most common occurrences that I see as a therapist and one of the most important life lessons to fully embrace. You may be struggling with an unfulfilling job or dysfunctional, unsatisfying relationship and you've tried countless ways to make things better. Sadly, your strategies don't seem to be working. The more they don't work and don't give you the results you are looking for, the harder you dig in your heels and increase your efforts with those *same* strategies. The thinking is, if you try hard enough you'll get the outcome you want.

Ironically, if something isn't working doing it more and harder will never change the outcome. It will only increase your frustration and feelings of helplessness and failure. If a round peg doesn't fit in a square hole, no matter how much you push and shove it will never fit. The issue is not about the amount of effort or energy you're putting into the task. It's really about are you putting in the *right* effort and energy into the *right* task?

27

When what you're doing isn't working it's often not a conscious process to up the ante and do it more and harder. Therefore you often have to completely stop and take a giant step back in order to decide whether or not you're taking the appropriate action to get what you need. The ways in which you respond to life's challenges may be more connected to doing what feels *familiar* but not necessarily what is the most effective course of action for a particular situation. Relying on the comfort of what feels familiar can keep you locked in a pattern of doing the same thing more and harder rather than stepping out of your comfort zone and seeking a new course of action.

It's useful to understand what your typical strategies are when you want to achieve something or attempt to change the outcome. Do you throw all of your weight into it and go at it full force? If you take this approach you may not realize that what you're doing isn't working well. Attacking like a bull in a china shop can yield dangerous results because it means you're coming at things with blinders on and have lost the ability to accurately assess the effectiveness of your actions or the outcome. Your angry state can cloud your judgment and certainly puts other people on the defensive so they're less likely to hear your concerns or want to work with you. This often creates a frustration that simply leads to more attacking.

Do you attempt to manipulate the situation in a more passive way? Being passive doesn't mean you aren't doing it "more and harder," it just means you're doing it in a more subtle, less obvious way. You're still wasting energy! Do you fall back and turn over all of your power to other people? This can create intense frustration and resentment as you watch *them* do it more and harder with no better results.

Other ways to do it "more and harder" might include ignoring other people's boundaries, stepping on their toes, and attempting to manage every aspect of a situation. You might be someone who only considers the big picture or becomes hyper-focused and lost on one small aspect of the issue. In any case you're probably beating a dead horse by staying rigidly focused on only one approach and not letting yourself consider a new perspective.

Another strategy to consider is whether you're constantly gathering other resources and running the risk of getting overwhelmed with too many opinions or options. If you can't make a decision, asking five more people to weigh in or reading 10 more books on the subject will only further complicate your decision-making process. Or you might do the opposite by always approaching issues and challenges alone. If you do you'll continually feel in the dark and anxious. Isolating yourself and refusing the input, guidance, and support of other people will not rid you of your anxiety or help you effectively meet that challenge head on.

The truth is any of the strategies I've mentioned can occasionally yield results when applied in the right circumstances. And all of them can be doomed to fail if you stay rigid and refuse to consider other options if what you're doing isn't working. The key is being flexible. Let go of the idea that there's only one way—your kneejerk response or most comfortable response—to achieving your goals. When something doesn't work, don't do it more and harder. Do something else!

And here's one more life lesson for you in regards to this issue: Sometimes no matter what you do or how hard you try, you won't influence or change the outcome at all. This is because there may be other external factors that are completely out of your control. You may be able to identify the pieces that are not in your control and in that case shift your focus and evaluate where it makes sense to put your efforts. Sometimes those variables may remain unknown to you. Learning to accept and make peace with that fact is just as important as not doing something more and harder when it doesn't work.

Questions For Continued Growth

———— * ————

1. What are your typical strategies when you want to change something in your life?

_____

_____

_____

_____

_____

_____

_____

_____

2. What's the extent to which you've continued to do something that's not working—more and harder—hoping for a different outcome?

_____

_____

_____

_____

_____

_____

_____

_____

3. What impact does it have when you keep getting the same unsatisfying results?

_____

_____

_____

_____

_____

_____

_____

_____

_____

4. What could you begin to do differently in order to get different results?

_____

_____

_____

_____

_____

_____

_____

_____

_____

5. What resources would you need to call upon to change your course of action?

_____

_____

_____

_____

_____

_____

_____

_____

_____

_____

6. List three things in your current life that you could stop trying to do more and harder.

_____

_____

_____

_____

_____

_____

_____

_____

You Can't Give Up An Unhealthy Behavior Until You Have Something to Replace it With

There's a wide range of behaviors that can be labeled "unhealthy." Although they tend to serve the purpose of comforting or numbing in the short term they typically lead to feelings of guilt or shame in the long-term. This is because on some level it's understood that despite the immediate gratification of relief or soothing, ultimately whatever strategy you're engaging in is negatively impacting your physical, social, emotional, or psychological well-being and safety. Oftentimes behaviors—including eating disorders, substance abuse and other addictions, acts of self-mutilation and other high-risk acts of self-endangerment—create tension in personal relationships, increase isolation and secrecy, and start to feel like they're controlling you and even taking over your life.

There may have been a time in your past when you attempted to let go of an unhealthy behavior. Perhaps you were motivated by the fact that the behavior left you feeling guilty, ashamed, or helpless. Maybe you felt pressured by a loved one giving you an ultimatum to either stop the behavior or risk losing the relationship. Oftentimes these behaviors become so consuming that they significantly interfere with workplace or academic performance or compromise your ability to be an effective and emotionally available parent, friend, or partner.

Like most people what you probably experienced in your well-meaning attempts to give up the behavior was the incredible difficulty of going "cold turkey." Even if you succeeded in abruptly stopping the behavior, you probably were faced with the additional challenge of sustaining your recovery by managing your cravings and impulses and not falling quickly back into a relapse. Although the intention of giving up a destructive behavior is a great sign of strength and courage, it's unreasonable and counterproductive to pursue that goal until you've first gained enough insight about the powerful factors that fuel and maintain your actions.

It's important to identify *why* you do the behavior before you can let it go. There are many reasons why people engage in self-harm. It can distract or numb you from other more painful memories or life events. When upsetting or unresolved experiences resurface in your life, turning to things like food, alcohol, shopping, Internet porn, or chaotic relationships all serve the purpose of pushing away or deadening overwhelming feelings and redirecting your thoughts and energy to something else.

Sometimes doing something self-destructive is intended to get emotionally unavailable people to notice your pain and reach out to offer you comfort, assistance, or compassion. Teenagers often use self-harming behaviors to get disconnected and distracted parents to re-engage with them.

If you have a history of trauma, abuse, or neglect and you don't have words to express those experiences the self-harm "shows" the pain you carry through your acting out behaviors. You might engage in behaviors that endanger your body to "punish" it because you wrongly hold it "responsible" for past abuse. Whatever the reason, these unresolved feelings and experiences need to be reconciled in other ways before it will feel right to let go of your existing coping strategies.

For anyone who turns to an addiction or self-destructive act there are always situations and circumstances that set the behaviors in motion by "triggering" upset feelings that inevitably lead to the decision to self-harm. Gaining insight about your personal triggers and understanding the relationship dynamics, challenging situations, or unsafe environments that set in motion the need to self-harm is another important step to address before the behavior can be changed. Once you can identify your personal triggers you'll be better prepared to avoid those scenarios, limit your exposure to them, or seek guidance and support in successfully navigating them. This in turn reduces the need to numb or distract with something injurious to your well-being.

It's important to remember that all acts of self-harm work in the short-term with a "payoff" of self-soothing, temporarily relieving anxiety, quieting overwhelming thoughts, communicating forbidden trauma narratives, or garnering the attention of an unavailable significant other. The life lesson is that in order to let go of your self-destructive act you need to be able to accomplish those same goals in other, healthier ways.

The brave decision to give up any addiction, an eating disorder, acts of self-mutilation, and high-risk behaviors is more likely to work when you include the guidance of a compassionate, well-trained mental health professional to process and heal unresolved pain. And since you can't let go of one behavior until you replace it with a new one that is just as effective, albeit safer, it becomes necessary to learn new ways to manage overwhelming thoughts and feelings and to cope more effectively with life stressors and challenges.

Part of why it's important to recognize the *process* of letting go __ destructive behaviors is to avoid the feelings of disappointment, disapproval, and failure that come from others as well as yourself when you attempt to give up your coping strategies without the safety net of support and alternative methods. When loved ones understand that it's not a matter of simply pouring the alcohol down the drain, turning off the pornography video, finally deciding to eat all the food on your plate, or putting down the razor blade, they can provide you with the patient, compassionate, and hopeful support you deserve and need to truly recover.

Questions For Continued Growth

———— * ————

1. What are some of the self-destructive behaviors you've used in the past or currently use?

_____

_____

_____

_____

_____

_____

_____

_____

2. What are the situations that might trigger the impulse to self-harm?

_____

_____

_____

_____

_____

_____

_____

3. What are the short-term "payoffs" you get from your destructive behaviors?

_____

_____

_____

_____

_____

_____

_____

_____

_____

4. What are the long-term negative consequences you experience from your acts of self-harm?

_____

_____

_____

_____

_____

_____

_____

_____

_____

5. What could you begin to do differently to comfort or self-soothe in ways that don't create guilt or shame?

_____

_____

_____

_____

_____

_____

_____

_____

6. Identify a specific behavior you would like to give up and list some possible alternatives to that behavior. What do you think and feel when you identify those other options?

_____

_____

_____

_____

_____

_____

_____

* * * * *

PART 2

Relationships

Any exploration of the factors that promote growth and change versus the things that create an impasse should include a discussion about the role that relationships play. When you're connected to healthy, safe, and loving people you feel their support and encouragement. Their words and their presence help to build your self-confidence, increasing the likelihood that you'll take healthy risks that move you forward in life. When people "have your back" you know they're rooting for you and will be there to catch you if you fall.

However, there are relationship dynamics that can sap you of precious energy, cause you to question your own worth, distract you, and prevent you from taking good care of yourself. In this section you can explore the extent to which you rely on others to confirm your worth, the value of your accomplishments, or the validity of your pain. Or you might discover you're focused on other people more than you realize and this has been compromising your ability to take good care of yourself.

It's not uncommon for people to compare themselves to others but rather than this being a source of motivation it's more likely that measuring yourself against others holds you back. Use these pages as an opportunity to take a closer look at the relationships in your life and find the courage to think about whether how you relate to others and how they relate to you supports or detracts from your personal growth.

You Don't Need Validation, Cooperation, or Apologies from Someone Else in Order to Heal

When you experience a hurtful or traumatic event that leaves you feeling helpless or without power part of what you hold on to is the idea that someone or something outside of you has a tremendous amount of control and you have none. Traumatic experiences including physical or sexual abuse, emotional neglect, or any threat to your safety or well-being are out of your control and it's normal to feel victimized by the person or situation that turned your world upside down and caused you harm.

In cases where the trauma is the result of a perpetrator's actions, it's common for survivors to believe that their healing can only occur when that same perpetrator takes responsibility for what they have done, expresses remorse, apologizes, and attempts to make amends. Unfortunately this logic leaves survivors in a never-ending state of being "at the mercy" of someone else. The abuser had all the power when they caused harm. They continue to have all of the power when it's believed they hold the key to whether or not healing can occur for the survivor.

After a lifetime of having your power or control taken away it might be confusing or hard to believe that the ability to heal lives inside of *you*. But despite your initial disbelief that your perpetrator doesn't have to contribute in any way to your healing allow yourself to be open to this possibility. And think about the corner you back yourself into when you hold on to the idea that you must get a confession of guilt and a heartfelt apology in order to move forward with your life.

It's worth knowing that much of the time perpetrators do not own their behaviors. At best they make excuses for and downplay what they've done and the impact it has had on you. At worst they remain in total denial, ridicule your pain, alienate you from family, or suggest that you're making up your accusations. Many abusers go to their graves in a state of denial without therapy, recovery, or healing of their own. As a result they're completely unable to give you what you need and deserve in terms of owning what they've done and the ways in which it has profoundly affected your life.

Even in situations where a perpetrator does "see the light" and apologizes, it will either be hard to trust in the sincerity of that apology or wind up feeling unsatisfying and hollow to you. In this case you might mistakenly believe that the perpetrator needs to apologize again, or do some other gesture to help heal the pain that still lives within you. If you follow this reasoning you're keeping alive the idea that your abuser has the power and the answers, and you'll continue to stay connected to him or her, allowing them to take up "head space" in unhealthy ways.

Given the painful reality that most abusers do not fully admit to what they've done and their apologies are not forthcoming, where does that leave you? Waiting and wanting and further traumatized. Instead, what if you embraced the life lesson that your *healing* had nothing to do with your abuser? Maybe it's possible that everything you need to validate your pain, your memories, and your awareness of the profound ways in which the experiences altered your life can come from you! Can you see how this would completely free you from the perpetrator's hold on you? This takes the power away from him or her and gives the power and control back to you.

Although there's healing that comes from feeling that your experiences have been "witnessed" and understood by compassionate, non-judgmental people in your life, this is still the icing on the cake. The most important part of healing comes from your own inner voice and the genuine personal belief that your perpetrator had no right to hurt you and was wrong in doing so.

Like many other survivors, the apology that you yearn for and the healing it creates can be internally felt when you, as a compassionate and loving adult, tell your own wounded "inner child" that you are "So sorry you were hurt." The concept of an "inner child" means visualizing yourself at a younger age and imagining that part of you still holds on to the feelings and memories associated with being hurt. It sometimes helps to look at a picture of yourself at a young age so you can get a mental image of that younger part of you.

When you imagine reconnecting with your younger self in your mind's eye and you express sorrow for the hurt that you experienced it doesn't mean that you're holding yourself responsible in any way for the trauma. Rather, you are expressing a gentle and kind awareness that something deeply harmful occurred and it was completely unfair.

The need to have your abuser take ownership for the pain they inflicted is universal and understandable. Yet it often doesn't happen. This legitimate need can be softened and released when you let that inner child know that *you* believe their pain is real and worthy of comfort and healing. And as I have stated before in this book, the one person and the only person you can ever control is you. You know the words you need to hear. You know what would be most soothing. And since you have the ability to say those words in a loving and truly effective way, they can have more impact than anything your perpetrator might say.

This idea also applies when the person who has hurt you is someone who is fundamentally loving and safe: your partner, good friend, sibling, or child. When one of those people unintentionally hurts you with unkind words, a disapproving look, or a behavior that runs counter to your needs, it's still reasonable to want that person to take ownership and apologize. And yet the same concept holds true: your well-being and inner peace can't be based upon their cooperation or compliance. They may come through and say all the right things. They may mean well but fall short. Or they may not believe that you're due an apology. Ask for what you need in relationships that are trust-worthy and emotionally safe, but recognize that you can move forward whether that person cooperates or not.

Questions For Continued Growth

— * —

1. Describe a time when you believed you needed someone else's cooperation in order to feel better or heal.

_____

_____

_____

_____

_____

_____

_____

_____

_____

2. What happened when you didn't get their cooperation?

_____

_____

_____

_____

_____

_____

_____

_____

3. How could letting go of the need for their cooperation or an apology set you free in your life?

_____

_____

_____

_____

_____

_____

_____

_____

4. What would you need to do in order to stop looking outward for that cooperation or apology?

_____

_____

_____

_____

_____

_____

_____

_____

5. What words of comfort could you give to yourself to assist in your ability to move forward?

_____

_____

_____

_____

_____

_____

_____

_____

6. Imagine letting go of the need to get an apology from someone who hurt you and describe how you feel when you sit with that idea.

_____

_____

_____

_____

_____

_____

_____

Don't Downplay Your Accomplishments by Comparing Them to the Successes of Others

It's amazing how difficult it is for people to allow their successes to stand on their own. Whether they are big or small, the natural tendency is to immediately measure one's accomplishments against someone else's, using that as the yardstick to decide whether or not their achievement matters. There are several reasons why focusing on the accomplishments of other people doesn't make sense and is harmful to your self-esteem and self-worth.

In most instances the comparison is apples and oranges. Believe it or not just because someone is the same age as you, seems to be at the same place in life, or has accomplished something similar, doesn't mean there is any real basis for comparison. Perhaps you didn't get to "hit the ground running," the way they did. Maybe they had a lot more emotional support in realizing their goals. Maybe the availability of resources was totally different. They may have accomplished the same goal many times in the past while you have bravely attempted it for the very first time.

Sometimes when people measure their successes against someone else's accomplishments they aren't even using an equal peer as a point of reference. Although it can be inspiring to "look up to" a highly accomplished person it's unfair to compare yourself to someone who has a well-practiced skill set or who truly operates from a different level of ability than yours. There's always a backstory to someone else's achievements. Often it's unknown to anyone other than the person who has realized that goal. Therefore it doesn't make sense to judge and compare the finished product. The roads that were travelled to reach what seems to be the same end may be markedly different and varied.

The reason why it can be so harmful to compare yourself to others is that, typically, it only serves the purpose of *minimizing* or downplaying your accomplishments. Why would you want to undermine your efforts and your achievements by measuring them against another person's? It's worth being curious about that question in an attempt to gain some insight about the deeper motivation attached to your behavior. Beating yourself up for not "measuring up" will never help you get ahead. In fact, it's far more likely to frustrate and anger you, which typically has the effect of setting you back and *decreasing* your chances of succeeding.

It's possible that you had the experience of being compared to other people when you were younger and it got normalized for you. It's not unusual for parents to either subtly or overtly compare siblings and their accomplishments. Teachers and coaches often do the same thing to their students and athletes. Kids are often pitted against each other by making them aware of everyone's test scores and athletic accomplishments, and they're constantly reminded of where they stack up in relation to one another.

Even in adulthood, supervisors compare and announce the workplace performance of employees to keep everyone on their toes, reminding them that no one is indispensable while pushing them to produce more. Rather than acknowledging the unique accomplishments of each employee, organizations often subtly pit co-workers against each other, encouraging competition and gauging successes by measuring them against someone else's past or present performance.

Maybe whatever you attempted either in childhood or adulthood was repeatedly compared to the achievements of others in an effort to motivate you to try harder or excel. But focusing on what others have done takes the spotlight off of you and your efforts, and almost never succeeds in being motivational. It really just humiliates and shames.

The comparison game is a way to highlight where you fell short or how someone else rose above you. It's unusual for people to compare their deeds to someone else's and come out of that process focusing on how they trumped the other person's achievements. And if the focus does shift to "besting" someone else, that's not a mindset that is gracious or cooperative. So again, the only real purpose that thinking serves is to either make you feel inferior, incompetent, or superior, compared to your peers. It also makes the notion of achievement combative and competitive rather than something to celebrate in its own right.

So consider the life lesson of giving yourself permission to fully acknowledge your own accomplishments without comparing them to anyone else's. Let go of the idea that they have to be measured against and be better than someone else's deeds in order to count. And if you are raising children, consider the importance of helping them to master the same skill, particularly in regards to either competing with siblings or peers. It's not about what anyone else has done. Let each success stand independently of anyone else's, and give it its full due. Being able to celebrate small and large successes without minimizing them is the best form of motivation and the key to achieving additional growth and success.

Questions For Continued Growth

—— * ——

1. Which of your typical accomplishments tend to get downplayed when you compare them to the accomplishments of other people?

_____

_____

_____

_____

_____

_____

_____

_____

_____

2. What impact does that have on you emotionally, physically and behaviorally?

_____

_____

_____

_____

_____

_____

_____

_____

3. How do the significant people in your life tend to respond to your accomplishments? What impact do their responses have on you?

_____

_____

_____

_____

_____

_____

_____

_____

4. List three personal accomplishments that you can fully acknowledge without minimizing or comparing to other people.

_____

_____

_____

_____

_____

_____

_____

_____

5. List three specific ways in which you can celebrate them.

_____

_____

_____

_____

_____

_____

_____

_____

_____

6. Describe the thoughts, feelings, and sensations on your body when you let yourself fully celebrate your successes.

_____

_____

_____

_____

_____

_____

_____

_____

_____

Stop Worrying about What Other People Think of You— They're Too Busy Worrying about What Everyone Thinks of Them!

This really is one of the great ironies of life and relationships. You're certainly not alone if you find yourself walking into a room, social event, one-on-one meeting, or public gathering and immediately start focusing on what other people might be thinking about you. It's human nature to have fleeting thoughts about how others might see you, judge you, or respond to you. However, a higher degree of self-consciousness is much more anxiety producing and draining for people who struggle in some way with feelings of inadequacy, incompetence, internal shame, or guilt.

Worrying about the assessments that other people make can prevent you from showing up at the party, adult education class, job interview, board meeting, or first date. Your thoughts about the ways in which you might be judged can lead to crippling self-doubt, creating a self-imposed censorship that doesn't allow you to dress the way you want, pursue your passions, befriend the people you like, express an opinion, set a limit or boundary, or raise an objection.

In essence you stop being your "truest self," and instead live your life and express yourself in ways that you believe will get you the approval and acceptance of others. When you worry less about what other people think, it frees you up to connect with your own feelings and insights from your "truest self."

And here's where the irony comes in; most of the time, people in your life are intensely preoccupied with their own insecurities and concerns about being judged. This, in turn, means that they're unaware of the things you believe they're totally focused on about you!

When you go to that party and worry, non-stop, about everyone zeroing in on your pimple, you probably don't realize that every other person at that party is preoccupied with the negative or embarrassing "thing" they assume everyone else is noticing about them! Therefore it's no wonder that most people could really care less about whatever you imagine they're caring about. Focusing on their own pimples will trump your pimple every time! The sad part is so much energy is being spent worrying about one's "defective self."

It's true that there are people in the world who really do take pleasure in noticing other peoples' weaknesses or shortcomings. They like to gossip about it or cruelly point it out in an effort to embarrass or shame. Try to remember that anyone who does this and takes delight in it is typically using that strategy in an effort to feel better about themselves and their own shortcomings. Focusing on your "deficit" is a way to take the attention off of and distract away from their own. The less comfortable they feel in their own skin the more likely they are to criticize other people.

This is also an opportunity to make personal decisions about how much weight and power you're going to give the things you think are embarrassing about yourself. It can be quite freeing to acknowledge the "pimple" and then make a conscious decision to put it in perspective, even "let it go" and not let it ruin your day.

The less focused you are on your "weaknesses" or "shortcomings" the less you'll worry about what other people think of them.

As you go through life, you'll discover more and more that it's not possible to have everyone's approval. Once you realize that you don't *need* to win over everyone's approval in order to be okay, then what other people think becomes less and less important. Try to keep in mind the life lesson that most of the time we're all preoccupied with our own stuff, and people typically spend more energy judging themselves than they do judging other people.

The other part of that life lesson is that the less you judge yourself, the less judgmental you will be towards others. Compassion is a two-way street; the more you apply it to yourself the more you can see others through a similar lens. Imagine being able to walk into a social situation freed up to feel good about yourself and, therefore, to be able to focus on the positive qualities of others as well! It's a healthy mindset to strive for and can greatly enhance your experience of comfortably being in the world.

Questions For Continued Growth

—— * ——

1. How have your concerns about what people think of you held you
   back in life?

   _____

   _____

   _____

   _____

   _____

   _____

   _____

   _____

   _____

2. What do you imagine would happen if you spent less energy
   worrying about what people thought of you?

   _____

   _____

   _____

   _____

   _____

   _____

   _____

3. What would you be freed up to do if you stopped worrying about what other people thought of you?

_____

_____

_____

_____

_____

_____

_____

_____

4. What are the ways in which you judge other people?

_____

_____

_____

_____

_____

_____

_____

_____

5. What would shift or change in your life if you spent less time judging other people?

_____

_____

_____

_____

_____

_____

_____

_____

_____

6. Identify three personal strengths that you can focus on rather than worrying about your "deficits."

_____

_____

_____

_____

_____

_____

_____

_____

_____

No One Can Make You Feel Anything— What You Feel Is Your Choice

This life lesson is often a difficult one for people to fully grasp or believe. It's a commonly held idea that when an important person in your life says or does something that you disagree with their words or actions will "make" you feel angry, disappointed, frustrated, afraid, guilty, etc. Like everyone else, in early childhood you were taught to believe that people had the power to manipulate and control how other people felt. When you misbehaved your well-meaning parent probably said, "You make me so angry!" or "Don't make me come upstairs!" If you overheard a parent talking about another adult relationship in their life you probably heard them say, "She makes me so mad!' or "He's making me feel guilty."

In subtle but powerful ways you learned that other people have the ability to influence and dictate moods and behaviors. It initially can be disorienting to realize that no one can make you feel anything. The significant people in your life will certainly make statements and engage in all kinds of behaviors in an attempt to get you to feel certain emotions, but the extent to which you do or don't buy into their efforts is completely up to you.

See if the following illustrations make sense to you. Someone you care about is relentlessly waving a "guilt ticket" at you, inviting or pressuring you to "get on the bus" and take the guilt trip. They can put tremendous energy into waving that ticket in your face and that can certainly be uncomfortable, but no matter how hard they work at it the choice to actually get on the bus and take the guilt trip is *yours* to make.

A different person in your life puts on boxing gloves and tries to bully you to "get you in the ring" with them. Bobbing and weaving, they beckon you with their gloved fist, aggressively demanding that you enter the ring. And although that, too, can be trying, the decision to glove up and join them in the ring for that fight is entirely up to you.

In the first example a significant other wants you to feel guilty for something you've said or done or forgot to say or do. It's important to remember that you have many options in terms of how you feel about the situation. In almost all cases when someone else tries to make you feel guilty it's not productive and rarely leads to meaningful growth or change. Without feeling guilty you could choose to take ownership of your behavior, acknowledge the impact it had, and, depending upon the situation, either make amends or attempt to explain your perspective.

In the case of someone who is trying to make you feel angry you have the right to decide whether or not it's warranted or will serve a useful purpose. Again, the emphasis is on the realization that no one can "make" you feel anything, nor do you have the power to make others feel what they feel. When someone is being difficult or antagonistic remind yourself that even though you can't control his or her behavior you *can* control the impact it has on you. You can choose to get angry in return or you can choose to stay calm or even request a time-out to temporarily walk away from the situation until you both calm down.

This is a useful life lesson to embrace. If you revert back to the belief that you can control what others feel or that they have the ability to "make" you feel your emotions, the idea of free choice and who actually has power in any given situation becomes confused and distorted. Ultimately *you* have the final say in what you do and don't feel; when you fully believe that, it gives you the opportunity to be even more mindful of your emotional choices.

Keep in mind that with this awareness comes responsibility. This means that if you chose to respond in ways that are emotionally or behaviorally negative or even harmful to another person you are fully accountable for your actions as well as the outcome; they didn't "make" you respond inappropriately. No one forces you to hit or push them, or be verbally unkind, regardless of what they do. That choice is yours and yours alone.

By the same token when someone else chooses to respond with verbal or physical hostility, impatience, or a lack of understanding and compassion they own that choice and the subsequent outcomes, not you.

Although it might sound like nothing more than a shift in language it's quite meaningful to go from "You make me angry," to "I choose to respond to you with anger." The first statement is a way to give up responsibility and control. The second statement is a reflection of the actual power that you possess in your relationships and in response to the varied situations that you encounter.

Questions For Continued Growth

———— ✳ ————

1. What were the messages you got in the past about people taking or not taking responsibility for their emotions?

_____

_____

_____

_____

_____

_____

_____

_____

2. Describe a time when someone tried to make you feel responsible for their emotional or behavioral responses.

_____

_____

_____

_____

_____

_____

_____

_____

3. Describe a time when you believed someone else made you feel what you felt.

_____

_____

_____

_____

_____

_____

_____

_____

_____

4. What did they do or say that led you to believe they were controlling your emotional response?

_____

_____

_____

_____

_____

_____

_____

_____

_____

5. How can you think about your emotional response in ways that give you back both responsibility and control?

_____

_____

_____

_____

_____

_____

_____

_____

_____

6. In the future, what can you say in response to someone who claims that you've made them feel a certain way?

_____

_____

_____

_____

_____

_____

_____

_____

_____

You Can Only Help Others When You Take Care of Yourself

There are so many religious, cultural, and family-based messages that emphasize how important it is to help or take care of other people. You may be caring for your dependent young child, a confused or challenging teenager, an elderly or ill parent, members of your faith community, the people you interact with every day in your job as a helping professional, or someone in need halfway around the world. Oftentimes if you are a deeply caring person it's all of the above!

Although you will be greatly admired for your efforts, there may not be any emphasis placed on the extent to which you're also taking care of yourself. In fact, this part of the equation tends to get totally ignored. And yet it's nearly impossible to be effective and to sustain your ability to nurture and help other people if you're not staying mindful of *your* needs as well. When you feel exhausted, resentful, or overwhelmed, consider the strong possibility that you're unable to give anything else to those around you because you haven't adequately paid attention to your own emotional and physical well-being.

If you're like a lot of other people this concept will seem somewhat foreign to you. How can you focus on yourself and focus on others at the same time? Actually, the first step is to focus on you! Making sure that you're getting enough sleep, eating properly, giving yourself time to play or just relax, strengthening your stamina with exercise, and connecting to spiritual resources are important ways to energize, unwind, and refuel.

When you make the time to do those things for yourself your ability to be there for other people increases. Keep in mind that you can only give what you have; in order to give more to others you have to first give to yourself. If you aren't taking the time to put more water in your "well" when others come with their buckets to draw from it, the well will be dry. If you only focus on helping other people you will eventually burn out.

The challenge is to live by this philosophy even when you don't have other people in your life who support it, or worse, continue to promote the idea that when you focus on yourself you're being "selfish." Making the time and taking the time to attend to your own emotional, physical, psychological, and spiritual needs is not selfish, it's *self-caring*.

But you might live from a powerful inner tape that reinforces the idea that there's something wrong with noticing, acknowledging, and attending to your feelings and needs. Take the time to understand where you were given the messages that play on the imaginary "tape recording" in your mind. Allow yourself to re-evaluate how accurate those powerful messages are in your life now. Ask yourself how you've benefitted from those core beliefs and find the courage to let go of the ones that attempt to make you feel guilty when you take care of *you*.

Be clear within yourself that you can only be truly effective and help others without resentment when you approach this goal from a rested, healthy place. Besides, it's so important to practice what you preach. If you believe other people are deserving of nurturance, support, resources, and connection, recognize that you're just as worthy!

When you don't practice self-care, yet insist that others engage in it, you're being hypocritical and can lose credibility in other people's eyes. It's a confusing double standard, particularly when you're trying to encourage a partner, child, or co-worker to do more self-care but don't model that philosophy through your own behavioral choices. One of the best ways to help others in their personal growth is to model a willingness to focus on that for you.

Questions For Continued Growth

*

1. While you were growing up what were the messages you received about self-care?

_____

_____

_____

_____

_____

_____

_____

_____

2. What are the messages you currently give to yourself about self-care?

_____

_____

_____

_____

_____

_____

_____

3. What happens to you emotionally and physically when you don't engage in self-care?

_____

_____

_____

_____

_____

_____

_____

_____

4. List three things you could do to increase the practice of taking care of yourself.

_____

_____

_____

_____

_____

_____

_____

_____

5. List three people in your life who can serve as role models for good self-care.

_____

_____

_____

_____

_____

_____

_____

_____

6. What would shift or change in your life if you increased your commitment to self-care?

_____

_____

_____

_____

_____

_____

_____

_____

Don't Invalidate Your Pain by Comparing It to the Experiences of Others

If you are like a lot of people you may find it difficult to acknowledge or honor any pain or trauma you have experienced. You might downplay what happened or the impact it has had on you. You might struggle to feel any sense of self-compassion for your hardships or minimize the courage and determination it took to get through your difficulties.

What often gets in the way of fully validating your experience is using other peoples' pain as a yardstick to measure the seriousness or importance of your own pain. It's interesting how easy it is to shift your focus and buy into the idea that if someone else has suffered a lot, your pain suddenly doesn't count.

The truth is it's really not useful to compare your life story or experiences to anyone else's. Your pain is yours. No matter how it looks on paper no one else can truly understand how that pain felt for you, the impact it has had throughout your life, or the meaning you attached to the experience. In the same way you can't fully know how someone else's pain has affected them, it isn't reasonable to make assumptions about it or measure it against your own experiences.

There can also be a lot of variables in painful experiences. It's one thing to suffer in some way—physically, emotionally, psychologically—it's another thing to suffer alone and without resources for support or comfort. People who have been sexually or physically traumatized and who blame themselves or were made to feel responsible might suffer differently than someone who doesn't take ownership of shame and blame.

Many people believe that witnessing something traumatic can't be as bad as experiencing it firsthand. This is often not the case. Witnessing can make you feel very complicated emotions. You might be haunted by your inability to have stopped what was happening. You might feel guilty for not rescuing the victim or even guilty about the fact that you were spared or survived what happened. This is another reminder that it doesn't make sense to judge painful experiences, compare, or make assumptions about them.

Ultimately, it is important to fully acknowledge your experience without apology or pretending it "wasn't so bad." The only way to fully heal from it is to allow it to exist, in and of itself, and to address all the thoughts and feelings that go with it, without downplaying or minimizing the significance or the impact.

And keep in mind that validating your pain never invalidates someone else's. Fully embracing the impact of your life experiences doesn't take away from their experiences. It's not supposed to be a contest or a win/lose situation. Everyone's experience is legitimate and you don't need to create a pecking order of "more or less important" or "more or less painful."

Questions For Continued Growth

— * —

1. While you were growing up how did the people in your life respond when you struggled or had a painful experience?

_____

_____

_____

_____

_____

_____

_____

_____

2. What words of comfort could you now give to yourself in response to a painful life experience?

_____

_____

_____

_____

_____

_____

_____

3. What words of comfort could you now give to yourself in response to a having witnessed a painful life experience?

_____

_____

_____

_____

_____

_____

_____

_____

4. In the past, if you downplayed a painful experience, why did it feel necessary to do that?

_____

_____

_____

_____

_____

_____

_____

_____

5. Who are the people in your life who believe that your experiences and emotions are worth acknowledging?

_____

_____

_____

_____

_____

_____

_____

_____

_____

6. What would those people say about the pain you've been through?

_____

_____

_____

_____

_____

_____

_____

_____

* * * * *

PART 3

Being in
The Present

The journey that you're on takes courage. To achieve personal and professional growth and make changes, large and small, requires a willingness to continually look at yourself and your life in order to understand what's working and what's not. When there are distractions, crises, fires to put out, and situations and other people to obsessively worry about it's hard to accurately recognize or address your own issues or areas for growth. Learning how to slow down and really experience each present moment as well as the cues your body gives you in response to those moments can be very challenging. And yet it is an essential part of the process.

In this section you'll be invited to consider the value and importance of living in the moment. This involves a conscious decision to be less busy and more focused on the practice of stillness. When you give yourself permission to slow down enough you will notice a greater connection to the world around you and to your own body. You'll have a deeper understanding of what you feel and what you need. You'll be better able to celebrate your successes and achievements rather than quickly moving on to the next goal.

The notion of "slowing down" can be scary; distractions serve many purposes and it's useful to understand the role they play in your life. Additionally, as you cultivate the ability to be more in the present moment you will notice an increase in gratitude. It's hard to be grateful for the things that fly past you. Slowing down allows you to savor the beauty in nature, the miracles that unfold every day, the acts of kindness performed by loved ones and strangers, the fact that you're a survivor!

Being in the present moment helps you monitor where you are in your own growth process and enables you to acknowledge new choices, behaviors, and thoughts. Being in the present moment lets you celebrate your progress, and this will motivate you to keep going and keep growing.

Do Less, Feel More

This is an interesting and simple idea, yet so many people have never connected these two concepts. If you're someone who lives in a constant state of "doing" it's worth being curious about why it sometimes feels challenging to "power down" and do less. "Constantly doing" means keeping yourself in never-ending motion. That can play out at work when you consistently put in extra hours, take on new projects, volunteer beyond your job description, cover for co-workers, or bring work home with you every night. You might dismiss the thought of slowing down or taking a break because you feel pressured or burdened to stay on top of or a step ahead of your workplace responsibilities.

It can also manifest in personal relationships when you run around with an invisible "water hose," putting out the complicated "fires" in other people's lives. You might financially or emotionally rescue or enable others by taking the fall for them or protecting them from experiencing the consequences of their own actions because you don't want them to suffer. Or you might spend a lot of time in caretaker mode, generously giving to others while you ignore your own needs.

Sometimes the constant motion is just latching onto people, places, and things that are nothing more than time-consuming distractions like getting caught up in high drama, or surfing the Internet for countless hours with no real purpose or focus. In this digital age it's so easy to waste time online preoccupying your mind with meaningless video games, chat rooms, or articles on the latest gossip. It's amazing how easy it is to lose track of time when you're somewhat hypnotized by the words and images on a computer screen.

Some people keep busy by preoccupying themselves with thoughts that don't go anywhere or ever get resolved. Worrying can take up huge amounts of time. Replaying conversations or past experiences and feeling bad about them can be totally consuming, and never changes anything. If you're like a lot of people you might do the "what if" or "if only" game. "What if I had done that differently?" "If only I'd made that choice instead." This can needlessly overwhelm you and make you feel a little crazy in the process! And no matter how much you focus on it, it never changes anything.

The thing to be curious about is *what are you trying to avoid* as you intensely keep yourself occupied and in overdrive? And here's where the idea that "when you do less you feel more" comes into play. When you slow your body down and allow yourself to be even temporarily present or still, invariably that creates an opening inside. This opening can potentially connect to memories, feelings, and experiences that are uncomfortable, or even scary and overwhelming. So consider the strong possibility that your constant movement might be a way to avoid getting close to a memory, feeling, or reality check about a current situation that's hard to manage. Whether you realize it or not, you have cleverly found a way to avoid going there by always going somewhere else.

Yet when you find the courage to slow down you can begin to identify what it is that causes you discomfort. Naming the problem is the first step towards being able to do something about it. Once you have the insight and the awareness you can start to come up with strategies about what to do. What behaviors need to change? What do you need to let go of or attend to with more commitment? Where would your energies really best be served?

Until you trust that you can handle whatever those unresolved feelings and experiences are it's understandable that you will feel forced to distract yourself. In fact, the more intense distractions can lead to mental, emotional, or physical exhaustion, which becomes another way to avoid dealing with whatever frightens you. Find the courage to believe that when you do choose to become still and the memories and emotions resurface you can find the inner strength, combined with the necessary outer resources and support that you deserve, to manage and work through whatever you have been running from.

In fact, the faster you run, the bigger those demons become. Avoidance can hold you hostage and make you feel more afraid. Take the first step and slow down, even a little bit. Notice what happens and trust you can handle it. If whatever comes up feels uncomfortable, think about using healthy self-soothing strategies, which include reaching out to others to ease the pain, rather than depleting yourself further by going back into overdrive. If you don't slow down you'll never be able to name, work through, and resolve the sources of your discomfort. Sooner or later you'll be running on empty and that will only create new problems for you.

Questions For Continued Growth

— * —

1. Describe the conversation you have in your head when you consider the possibility of slowing down.

_____

_____

_____

_____

_____

_____

_____

_____

2. Identify a time when you were able to slow down. What was that like for you?

_____

_____

_____

_____

_____

_____

_____

3. When you did slow down what shifted or changed in your daily life, workplace, or relationships?

_____

_____

_____

_____

_____

_____

_____

_____

4. If slowing down feels very challenging, why do you think it's so hard?

_____

_____

_____

_____

_____

_____

_____

_____

5. What would it take to overcome those obstacles?

_____

_____

_____

_____

_____

_____

_____

_____

6. If you expended less energy running on empty, what would you do instead?

_____

_____

_____

_____

_____

_____

_____

_____

Live in the Present Moment

It's not a coincidence that so many people in our country suffer from either depression or anxiety. Depression is often experienced as profound feelings of sadness, helplessness, hopelessness, guilt, and low self-esteem. Often these relate to being stuck in the past. Sometimes it connects to a sense of regret, believing you should have accomplished more things in your life, or holding on to guilt about things you've done in the past. Sometimes it's fueled by the loss of something or someone who is no longer with you, as in the case of profound grief or bereavement.

If you have a prior history of trauma or abuse there can be an ongoing, frozen, almost childlike feeling of victimization, or the belief that you have to keep using coping strategies that are rooted in the past in order to be safe in the world. Those strategies might include not rocking the boat, staying small and silent, not trusting other people, or aggressively fighting to get your needs met. If you're a survivor of abuse you may relate to the feeling of depression that comes from being alone in your pain, or in not having had the opportunity to process or heal from what was done to you. All of these experiences and coping strategies can keep you wedded to the past.

If depression keeps you stuck in the past, feelings of anxiety are often fueled by the worry that comes from future-oriented thinking. Fears take the form of "what if" something bad happens. If you engage in excessive worry you're probably focused on something that hasn't actually occurred, but in your forward-thinking mind, you are coming up with possible bad outcomes. This can be an unconscious way to brace for inevitable danger or unpredictability. Without realizing it many people go through life attempting to prepare for the worst possible scenarios by obsessing about them. In actuality, obsessing about the unknown does nothing to help us prepare for it.

Whether you're always looking behind you and stuck in the past, or continually focusing on potentially negative outcomes in the future, the important point is you're clearly not in the present moment! The irony about living this way is that the past can never be undone or changed—no matter how much you think about it—and the future can never really be predicted—no matter how hard you try. So in both cases the energy you're spending is wasted.

However, that energy can serve you really well in the present! What is happening for you right now? What are the present-day experiences that are available to you? It's possible that some of the resources you need to soothe and heal past pains, or comfort you about future worries, are *currently* present in your life and aren't being accessed or used by you because you aren't noticing "now."

It's certainly true that you have the right to make peace with your past and that often means looking at it and working through it with support. You also have the right to feel prepared for the future, and that might require some thinking and planning. However, the best way to accomplish both of those goals is to be able to draw upon the resources and strengths that exist in the *present*.

Although you might not realize it and may need some assistance in seeing it, the present is filled with moments of beauty, joy, possibility, and hope. When you look around you you'll start to notice that there are people in your "present" who care and are available to you. There is your own inner wisdom that you can connect to in the present moment. There are insights and realizations that can surface and be revealed. There are external resources for guidance, feedback, support, coping, and validation.

All of these things can be completely missed if you're always looking behind you or way ahead. So allow yourself to consider the value of pausing and really being in "now." Try to not get frustrated or give up if this doesn't come easily or naturally at first. You've conditioned your mind to have tunnel vision about either the past or the future and it's where you've been "living" for a long time. You may have even convinced yourself that it was *safer* to live in the past or the future.

Being mindful and focusing on the present moment initially takes conscious awareness and work. Sit quietly for a moment and notice where your thoughts and feelings go. Then see if you can gently bring your awareness back, again and again, to the present moment. You can anchor yourself in the present by connecting with sensations on your body or the sights and sounds around you. Simply naming your present experiences can increase your awareness about them.

Practice bringing yourself back to the present moment and as you work on it be aware of keeping judgment or criticism out of the equation. That approach will not motivate you, and ironically, those emotions will actually increase depression or anxiety. In time it will become much easier to do and then you'll start to discover the gifts that are *here*, waiting to be noticed and used.

Questions For Continued Growth
—— * ——

1. Describe one incident that keeps you rooted in the past and compromises your being in the present moment.

_____

_____

_____

_____

_____

_____

_____

_____

2. What do you imagine would happen if you made the decision to let go of that past experience?

_____

_____

_____

_____

_____

_____

_____

3. Describe one future event that you worry about and that compromises your being in the present moment.

_____

_____

_____

_____

_____

_____

_____

_____

4. What do you imagine would happen if you made the decision to let go of that future worry?

_____

_____

_____

_____

_____

_____

_____

_____

5. Describe a present moment experience that you can focus on and enjoy instead.

_____

_____

_____

_____

_____

_____

_____

_____

_____

6. What are the thoughts, feelings, and body sensations that let you know you're truly in the present moment?

_____

_____

_____

_____

_____

_____

_____

_____

Celebrate When You Choose to Do What You're Supposed to Do

As a therapist I spend a lot of time complimenting my clients on the good choices they make. Their responses are remarkably the same. "Why are you complimenting me for something I'm *supposed* to be doing? If I *should* do it, then it really doesn't count, does it?" Is that an idea that you relate to as well? It's common for people to minimize their accomplishments if what they're doing is a natural part of their "job description" in life.

Parents are "supposed to be" loving. People who are employed are "supposed to" show up on time and do their jobs well. Students "should be" studying hard and getting good grades. Human beings "should" help one another and deal with each other compassionately. A husband or wife "should" communicate well and support one another. You get the idea.

And although everything I mentioned above *should* be the case, and in the best of all possible worlds those responsible behaviors would simply come to pass, being human and living the life you live makes it much more complicated than that. The real truth is, doing the "right" thing is a choice. And it's a choice that often takes effort, energy, and hard work. It's also a choice that can still create internal tension and uncertainty. Just because you "should" behave in specific ways doesn't mean it's always the easiest course of action. I strongly believe that the best way to reinforce these good choices and behaviors is to acknowledge them—both in others and in yourself.

Prior life events, your moods, exhaustion, temptations, distractions, and complicated circumstances can all move you away from doing the "right" thing. Therefore you need to get credit every time you rise above the "easier" way out and go the extra mile. Even when doing the "right" thing is easy for you, it's important to take a moment and allow yourself to genuinely feel good about it. Again, this will increase the likelihood that you will continue to make choices that are responsible, compassionate, or self-caring.

Ironically, when you minimize or ignore the fact that you've done the "right thing" you may actually decrease that behavior. By downplaying its significance you're saying it isn't really important and you'll probably be less likely to stay mindful of repeating it in the future.

At the end of the day you *choose* to be that loving parent or partner, the reliable and productive employee, the hard-working student, or the generous contributor to a worthy cause. It's important to acknowledge that choice and allow yourself to feel good about it.

It's equally important to acknowledge when someone in your life is making similar choices. Don't take for granted the fact that your partner spontaneously bought you flowers, or the babysitter didn't complain when you were an hour late getting home from work, or your teenager helped to clear the dinner dishes. Show them genuine gratitude. They *chose* to make the effort to do the right thing and should be positively reinforced for it. You'll discover that expressions of gratitude always create more positive choices!

As you read this notice how comfortably the idea of acknowledging good choices and positive behavior is for you. There can be strong childhood messages, often culturally reinforced, that look down on the idea of celebrating what we're "supposed" to do. The emphasis is typically placed on pointing out the times when someone falls short or screws up. If you grew up in a family that took for granted the times when you did well, respected others, lent a helping hand, or met your obligations, then this concept might seem quite foreign or even silly to you.

Sit with this for a bit. And find the courage to ask yourself how it would have felt if those things *had been* acknowledged as you were growing up. Is it possible that the positive reinforcement would have been helpful to your self-confidence and evolving sense of self-worth? If your good deeds had been celebrated would you have done them more often or less often? Is it possible that the lack of acknowledgement was actually discouraging and sometimes negatively affected your motivation? Did it ever create a feeling of resentment when your hard work went unnoticed?

If you discover that this mindset really was detrimental know that you have the power to repair it by consciously choosing to celebrate your big and small accomplishments from this point on. It won't make you cocky and it doesn't mean you're bragging. It will help to nurture a sense of purpose, pride, and validation that will increase your good works in the future.

Questions For Continued Growth

———— * ————

1. Describe a time when you chose to do the "right thing."

_____

_____

_____

_____

_____

_____

_____

_____

_____

2. How were you able to make that good choice?

_____

_____

_____

_____

_____

_____

_____

_____

3. List three concrete things you can do to celebrate your good deeds or good choices.

_____

_____

_____

_____

_____

_____

_____

_____

4. List three good choices your significant others have chosen to make.

_____

_____

_____

_____

_____

_____

_____

_____

5. What can you do to celebrate the good deeds or good choices your significant others make?

_____

_____

_____

_____

_____

_____

_____

_____

_____

6. What shift or changes would occur in your life if you complimented yourself on your good choices more often?

_____

_____

_____

_____

_____

_____

_____

_____

_____

Listen to the Uh-Oh Feeling in Your Stomach

One of the life lessons that might be challenging for you to accept is the notion that your body "talks" to you all the time. And believe it or not, the information and feedback it provides is important and remarkably accurate. Part of why this is hard to embrace is because society reinforces the idea of ignoring body sensations with messages that encourage you to "shake it off," take a pill to get rid of pain, or override discomfort with distractions.

"Listening" to your body also might be difficult to do if you grew up in a family that consistently ignored actual experiences that were going on in your home. When scary or threatening things unfolded your body let you know that you were potentially unsafe. Maybe you felt something stirring in your gut, it became hard to swallow, your chest felt heavy, your muscles tightened, or your breathing changed. Those were important "body cues" letting you know that something was wrong while simultaneously preparing you to respond to the threat in some way.

And yet as your body alerted you to danger and attempted to put you in survival mode, people you trusted told you "nothing is wrong," "you're overreacting," "you're being paranoid." Despite the fact that your body didn't lie and your instincts were right, those powerful and confusing messages created self-doubt. Over time as similar body sensations kicked in, you probably got really good at downplaying or ignoring them. The more you disconnected from your body and its physical messages, the more you invalidated one of your most important built-in assessment tools.

When you think about it it's fairly easy to censor your words, distract your thoughts, or suppress your emotions. However, sensations on the body show up whether you want them to or not. You can't manipulate your body into feeling or not feeling the aches, pains, tightening, numbing, tingling, jittery, hot, cold, heavy, or dizzy feelings that you experience. This is part of why you can trust that they serve as a kind of radar or compass, giving you insight about your levels of comfort, threat, connection, and safety in your relationships and in your environment.

Most people understand the notion of a "gut feeling." This is not just an expression, you really do experience profound feelings and sensations in your stomach and gut, and it's worth listening to those feelings as you contemplate a decision or weigh the strength of your instincts. It can be equally helpful to notice other sensations in different parts of your body as well. There is a whole "zone" of feeling that travels from the top of your head down to your gut and if you practice doing a body "scan" you will become more aware of the information encoded in that zone.

Imagine a Xerox machine with the light that slowly scans across a page to reproduce it. Now imagine that light slowly moving from the top of your head down your body. Notice sensations starting at the top of your head, moving down to your forehead, behind your eyes, down your face, to your jaw, throat, neck, shoulders, across your chest, draping behind your back, wrapping around your belly and traveling even lower to the pit of your stomach. Each one of those areas becomes a resource for information, letting you know if you're calm, frightened, aroused, anxious, angry, tired.

It can also be difficult to trust body sensations if experiences of sexual arousal and pleasure were paired with force, abuse, violence, domination, or victimization. It's profoundly confusing when you're sexually violated yet still experience a sexual response. This can create feelings of guilt and shame and cause you to again disconnect from and stop trusting your body sensations.

Many sexual abuse survivors say, "I know I didn't want what was happening to me, so why did my body still respond? It must mean that I can't trust my body." In actuality it's important to separate out the ways in which your body reacts to forced, unwanted stimulation that will still bring about a physical response from what your heart feels and your mind wants. But even in the case of victims who are being forced into arousal, there is still that all important "uh-oh" feeling in the pit of the stomach letting them know that what's happening is threatening or unwanted.

The irony is that the more you try to detach from the ways in which you experience uncomfortable feelings on your body, the more those feelings intensify exactly because you're ignoring them! Until you acknowledge and attend to the feelings they will probably stick around, continuing to cause you distress. So the life lesson is to allow yourself to reconnect with body sensations and trust that important information is being given to you through those physical experiences. Start to notice which part of your body is the most reactive as everyone tends to have vulnerable places that typically "hold" tension or other sensations. When you become aware of the tightening in your belly, the clenching in your jaw, or the heaviness on your chest ask yourself, "If that sensation could talk what would it be saying to me?" Allow yourself to "listen" to those physical manifestations, approach them with curiosity and compassion, and commit to being responsive so the feelings can begin to subside.

The message might be that you need more sleep, or your body needs food. It might be letting you know whether or not the person you're with or the situation you're in is safe for you. It might be the guiding force in an important decision or risk-taking behavior. It could be a wake-up call about needing to do more self-care, or the first indication of a medical or mental health scenario that needs your attention. Learn to listen to and respect your body. Understand that it works for your benefit, giving you a window into your truest needs and feelings.

Questions For Continued Growth

———— * ————

1. What are the past experiences that taught you to either trust or not trust your body's sensations?

_____

_____

_____

_____

_____

_____

_____

_____

2. Historically, how have you responded to the "uh-oh" feeling in your stomach?

_____

_____

_____

_____

_____

_____

_____

_____

3. In what other ways does your body let you know that something is not right for you?

_____

_____

_____

_____

_____

_____

_____

_____

4. What do you imagine would happen if you allowed yourself to pay attention to the sensations on your body?

_____

_____

_____

_____

_____

_____

_____

_____

5. If your body sensations could talk what would they say?

_____

_____

_____

_____

_____

_____

_____

_____

_____

6. List two ways in which you could bring comfort to your body.

_____

_____

_____

_____

_____

_____

_____

_____

_____

_____

Make Decisions from What Is Rather Than What Was or What Could Be

Whether you are conscious of it or not you may be making important life choices either from the past or the future rather than accurately assessing what the current realities are in your life. This is a dynamic that often relates to decisions about relationships. Despite the fact that many people express unhappiness about their partner's behavior or the current state of their relationship they still choose to stay. This is because they're remembering how satisfying it was *in the past* and holding on to those memories becomes a way to justify not leaving.

If you relate to this you might find yourself wistfully reminiscing about the good times you used to have or the upbeat and loving ways your partner used to behave. Rather than being in the present you may be traveling back in time to the earliest stages of your relationship: a time when most people are on their best behavior as they attempt to win over a prospective partner. As you cling to those recollections you hope those positive feelings and experiences return so the relationship can start to feel like it felt in the past.

If you're not dwelling on the past you may be looking to the future, holding out hope that at some point your partner will "see the light" or make the significant changes that would allow the relationship to reach a new level of fulfillment. It's not unusual to focus on a partner's "potential" and assume that whatever qualities you presume to be hidden within will eventually show themselves and dramatically alter their personality, emotions, or behaviors. Many people are willing to wait indefinitely for those changes to surface, continuing to believe that it's just a matter of time before they come to light.

In both cases tremendous weight is either given to what used to be or the promise of what could be. When you're not living in the present moment you're not taking into consideration the current circumstances that dictate your partner's moods and behaviors and the impact they have on the quality of your relationship and your life. Whatever is happening in the present is your best indicator of how things are and will continue to be rather than the hope that rests in digging up the past or banking on a better future.

That's not to say that you can't be optimistic about the capacity for growth and change. But as we've already discussed in other chapters, people only change when they want to, not because someone else insists upon it or tries to manipulate it into happening. When it comes to making choices about staying or leaving an unsatisfying relationship you deserve to have clarity about your partner's intentions rather than assuming the past can be relived or the future realized. As much as you might want those changes to take place it helps to check in with your partner to see if they have the same agenda. Their sense of the present might be quite different from yours.

It's understandable that some people revert to and focus on the past or the future so they don't have to feel the discomfort of the present. It takes courage to see your present reality for what it really is. But whatever is happening in the present can't be ignored forever. As difficult as it might be, sooner or later those are the issues and feelings that need to be addressed for true change to occur.

There are other important life decisions that sometimes get made from needs and emotions rooted in the past or circumstances connected to the future, rather than current reality. Whether you're making choices about where you want to live, the next step in your education, whether or not to start a family or have another child, or the kind of job or career you're pursuing and the workplace setting that would best support that, think about your present realities. These might include your current finances, the state of your medical and mental health, the degree to which you're connected to resources, and the availability of your external support system. You also should consider your access to transportation, present-day responsibilities and stressors, the current needs of other family members, childcare issues, and your level of physical fitness and stamina.

It's a wonderful thing to dream, to have future-oriented goals, and even to reminisce about past experiences that move you or evoke warm, sentimental feelings. Hold onto those memories and future dreams. And when it comes to the big decisions, the life lesson is to take an honest and realistic look at where you are and what's currently happening in your life because those will be the determining factors in how your choices play out.

Questions For Continued Growth

———— * ————

1. Identify something you're holding on to that's based upon how things "used to be."

_____

_____

_____

_____

_____

_____

_____

_____

_____

2. What might change for you if you made that choice based upon your present reality?

_____

_____

_____

_____

_____

_____

_____

_____

3. Identify something you're holding on to because of its future "potential."

_____

_____

_____

_____

_____

_____

_____

_____

4. What might change for you if you made that choice based upon your present reality?

_____

_____

_____

_____

_____

_____

_____

_____

5. Identify a current life choice that you could make from your current reality.

_____

_____

_____

_____

_____

_____

_____

_____

6. Describe what the process is like for you when you stay firmly rooted in the present.

_____

_____

_____

_____

_____

_____

_____

_____

Live Every Day
from a Place
of Gratitude

When you're confronted with and navigate difficult challenges in your life it's easy to lose sight of what there is to be grateful for on a daily basis. Even when positive events and interactions take place, it's more likely that those things are taken for granted, which also minimizes an awareness of gratitude. Although "being grateful" is a popular idea, many people struggle with putting the concept into actual practice.

In some families the notion of gratitude is never discussed or modeled. Like many other emotional states, feeling grateful in reaction to positive experiences is something that children are taught to feel. When primary caretakers never openly express gratitude because they operate from a sense of entitlement and *expect* to be continually showered with blessings, that positive modeling doesn't happen. With a mindset of entitlement, parents never pause to really pay attention to or acknowledge what they have.

It's also possible to grow up with people who stay rigidly focused on what they *don't* have in life. In those cases, anger and complaints continually override any feeling of gratitude. This can manifest as a "yeah, but" attitude. Whenever anyone attempts to point out a good thing that has happened or a gift they have in their life, there is an immediate shift to, "Yeah, but" that other good thing still hasn't happened and there are better things I still don't have yet!" "Yeah, but" always cancels out positive thoughts, teaching children to always keep the spotlight on what's missing rather than on what they've received.

For other people, gratitude can get tangled up with shame. Many parents create a sense of guilt in their children if their expressions of gratitude are not continuous, deeply heartfelt, or abundant enough. In those cases, demanding gratitude for every large and small parental gesture is more about the parent's need for ongoing validation, acknowledgment, and ego boosting, rather than a core value that's important to instill in children so they learn how to express thanks and appreciation for the blessings in their lives.

Parents who were traumatized in childhood and grew up without the love and safety they deserved become easily angered at their children for not fully appreciating "how much better they have it than I did." And yet it's unfair to expect children who are growing up with loving parents to compare their lives to the childhoods of their abused parents. All they know is the safety they experience, and they have the right to expect and assume that they'll continue to be treated lovingly.

Abusive or overly needy parents can demand their children express *excessive* gratitude for the basic things they deserve and should receive, including food, shelter, emotional and physical safety, attention, and love. In those cases the idea of being grateful becomes confusing, and implies that these basic necessities of life aren't really due to them. Although it's important to teach children to say, "thank you," those aforementioned experiences and resources should be givens in their lives.

When parents insist upon constant gratitude from their children the message is they're getting more than they deserve and more than what the parent needs to be offering. Parents are supposed to be safe, loving, available, and committed to meeting their child's basic needs. It's their obligation and responsibility as parents.

There's no question that experiences like depression, personal or societal traumas and tragedies, and illness or death can overshadow feelings of gratitude with feelings of loss, grief, terror, anxiety, hopelessness, and powerlessness. It can take a long time to go from those symptoms of post-traumatic stress to the feelings of gratitude that represent post-traumatic growth. Reaching a place of gratitude for *surviving* tragedy or trauma is a personal journey that unfolds differently for every individual who has suffered.

Beginning to notice the small, positive, or miraculous things in nature, personal relationships, your own being, or the larger world takes time and conscious effort. When there's been a lot of pain you can develop tunnel vision about your life, only focusing in on evidence of more pain. Changing the lens that you use to look at the world and other people takes practice. But one of the great life lessons is the fact that once you commit to noticing positive blessings, you see more of them and gratitude expands.

The honest truth about life is that there is *always* something to be grateful for. Your challenge and opportunity is to keep noticing the day-to-day experiences and encounters that support this idea. Try taking a "gratitude walk" in a safe and pleasing environment and say out loud a few things that bring up gratitude. Think about an important person in your life and list their qualities or the ways in which they support you. That can create a feeling of gratitude. Notice the ways in which your own body moves and works on your behalf and see if you can access a feeling of gratitude for that.

Think about your own diverse abilities, attributes, and many accomplishments. Pay attention to the food you are fortunate to eat and the little niceties or luxuries in your life that make things easier or more manageable.

And when you can, offer up little prayers of thanks in your mind. Document and own the blessings in your life through journaling. Express your gratitude to the cherished people in your life who love and care about you. As you build this gratitude practice you will notice significant, positive shifts in your mood and your mindset. Living from a place of gratitude creates hope, optimism, and joy. And it's powerful to know that *you* can increase those positive experiences in your life.

Questions For Continued Growth

——— * ———

1. Identify three things you can be grateful for in your current life.

_____

_____

_____

_____

_____

_____

_____

_____

2. Identify three things you can be grateful for that occurred in
   the past.

_____

_____

_____

_____

_____

_____

_____

3. What impact does it have when you notice those feelings of gratitude?

_____

_____

_____

_____

_____

_____

_____

_____

4. List three concrete things can you do to increase a gratitude practice.

_____

_____

_____

_____

_____

_____

_____

_____

_____

5. How could you express gratitude towards a loving and supportive person in your life?

_____

_____

_____

_____

_____

_____

_____

_____

6. What internal and external resources for support can you use to increase the likelihood of following through with a gratitude practice?

_____

_____

_____

_____

_____

_____

_____

_____

PART 4

* * * * *

Growth
and Change

The more you commit to looking inside of yourself the more you'll come to understand your strengths and abilities. You'll gain valuable insight about the thoughts, feelings, and behaviors that truly serve you well. You'll also have a better understanding about the ones that have been keeping you stuck, negatively affecting your self-esteem, keeping you in an unsafe or unfulfilling relationship or career. You're halfway home when you've opened your eyes and increased your level of self-awareness. You reach the finish line when you *act on* those newfound insights.

This can be a difficult part of the journey because it requires you to summon the courage to take actual steps in the direction of where you want to go. That means concrete movement to realize your goals even if you feel uncertain or afraid. It's not letting the normal anxiety or fear that is associated with change stop you from making those changes. It's about a willingness to act "as if" your dreams can become realities so you can access the thoughts, feelings, and choices that can make it so. It's finding the courage to stop doing the behaviors that have held you back even if they feel easy to hold on to.

It's also facing the realization that when things are calm and comfortable your level of motivation will go down. The most amount of change happens when there's the greatest degree of discomfort. This section of the book encourages you to turn unexpected events and difficult circumstances into opportunities for real growth and change.

At the same time it reinforces the idea that it's so important to focus your efforts and energies on the things that are within your power to change. Otherwise you're spinning your wheels and not putting enough effort into the things that really can be different for you. Hopefully the life lessons in this part of the book will motivate you to be proactive, to believe in your ability to work through your fears, and to take ownership of the behaviors that need to change.

Stop Apologizing and Start Changing Your Behavior

Don't get me wrong—apologizing is a necessary and very important thing to be able to do throughout your life. It takes courage and ego-strength to be responsible for and take ownership of your actions and to admit when you've made a mistake. Apologizing and, when needed, making heartfelt amends are essential ways in which you can help to heal the intentional or unintentional wounds you have inflicted upon others.

It may not surprise you to know that there are many people in the world who find it almost impossible to apologize. Pride, lack of role modeling, fear of appearing vulnerable, or the stubborn belief that there's nothing to apologize for are often the reasons why apologies aren't forthcoming. When you're unable to apologize to someone the wounding cuts even more deeply. That can make it much harder for people to forgive your actions and move on.

But there is another side to this story and it relates to people who are constantly apologizing for what they have said or done. The potential problem is that the apology becomes an excuse to speak unkindly or act poorly again and again in the future.

In other words there are lots of apologies but never any actual changes in behavior. Part of the mindset is, "As long as I eventually apologize, it's ok if I hurt others." In these cases the apologies are hollow and meaningless. They become a way to excuse and justify bad behavior.

It can be tricky when you're on the receiving end of what appears to be genuine words of regret. How can you *not* accept the apology? Doesn't that make you seem ungrateful or too harsh? And yet when the same behaviors happen again and again followed by the same apologies, it's legitimate to see the constant requests for forgiveness as manipulative and not genuine. You're within your rights if you become skeptical and find it impossible to accept those kinds of apologies.

The harder and more courageous thing to look at is whether *you* engage in a similar behavior. Think for a moment about the important relationships in your life. What are you most often apologizing for when you do apologize? Is there a recurring theme? How many times have you had to make amends for the same hurtful kinds of behaviors or insensitive words? Try to be brave enough to be honest with yourself, or if nothing comes to mind ask the significant people in your life if *they* can identify patterns to your apologies.

Now take the next mature step and work on reducing the apologizing by genuinely changing your behavior! Having to constantly apologize can take a toll on your sense of self-worth. It fuels the idea that you're messing up and can negatively impact your sense of yourself. It also takes a lot of effort to keep apologizing and you could re-channel that energy more productively by identifying concrete ways to change your behavior. When you dedicate yourself to being more sensitive to the thoughts, feelings, and needs of other people it enhances your sense of self-esteem.

Remember that constantly apologizing also affects how others see you. Over time you become the "boy who cried wolf" and your loss of credibility or sincerity can translate into other arenas of your life. People may see you as not being genuine, trustworthy, or sincerely caring about the ways in which you're hurtful. Stop yourself before launching back into old behaviors that inevitably get you into trouble because they disrespect or hurt other people. Ask yourself if there's another, kinder way you can express yourself or act.

When you notice yourself slipping back into older behavior patterns or saying something you know you will later regret, pause first and try to think more about the *impact* of your words or actions.

It's even a step in the right direction if you can pause midway through a hurtful sentence or an angry action and self-correct in that moment. Let the other person see that you've realized your mistake and you're actively working to make positive changes. People are quite willing to be patient and forgiving when they see you have more self-awareness and you're committed to growth and change.

When you do, these changes create a win-win for everyone!

Questions For Continued Growth

— * —

1. While you were growing up what messages did you get about apologizing for mistakes?

   _____

   _____

   _____

   _____

   _____

   _____

   _____

   _____

   _____

2. When people in your life apologize how sincere are their words? How do their behaviors change after the apology?

   _____

   _____

   _____

   _____

   _____

   _____

   _____

   _____

3. When you make a mistake or inadvertently hurt someone's feelings how easy it for you to apologize?

_____

_____

_____

_____

_____

_____

_____

_____

4. When you apologize how are your apologies received by others?

_____

_____

_____

_____

_____

_____

_____

_____

_____

_____

5. Identify one thing you repeatedly apologize for in your relationships.

_____

_____

_____

_____

_____

_____

_____

_____

6. How can you begin to change your behavior regarding that issue?

_____

_____

_____

_____

_____

_____

_____

_____

Put Your Energy Into Things You Can Truly Change

Think for a moment about how much of your time and energy you spend trying to fix or change other people or troubling situations in your life. Then gently ask yourself how much success you've achieved with these projects. If you're like most people you've spent countless hours trying to change someone's mind, help them to "see the light," or make an unworkable situation work. And yet your level of success is probably not that high!

This is not because you aren't clever or persistent enough, or that you still haven't found the magic key that unlocks the door or the missing puzzle piece that makes the picture complete. It's more likely that you're not "succeeding" because you continually try to change the things that are not in your power to change. As simple as that sounds it's a critically important realization. Until you're genuinely able to separate out who and what you can and can't change you'll probably continue to waste precious energy.

And while you keep trying to change the things you can't, you'll potentially fuel the mistaken idea that you have "failed" when change doesn't happen.

It can be a powerful exercise to assess how much time you're spending as you attempt to change something that's out of your control. In addition, think about the energy, emotions, thoughts, behaviors, and resources that get directed towards a project or a person that you really can't change. If you're like most people you get so caught up in your mission you lose perspective and don't realize how consuming those endeavors can be or the extent to which they keep you on a hamster wheel that has no resolution.

When you do recognize that your energy needs to be redirected towards the things that truly are within your ability to change it's both humbling and freeing. You might initially be disappointed when you realize that no matter what you say or do you're powerless over another person's behavioral choices. But it's also very freeing when you give yourself permission to stop needlessly spending that energy, and instead allow yourself to focus on what you really can control and change.

That brings up another important aspect of this life lesson: While you focus your efforts in the wrong directions you might not be putting *enough* energy and effort into the things that genuinely are within your ability to change. As a great rule of thumb know that you have the ability to change yourself and only yourself. When you focus on *your* thoughts, feelings, and actions you can allow yourself to re-evaluate whether or not they're effective, productive, and healthy.

Taking the time to do that creates the opportunity to strengthen what is working well, and that allows you to feel a sense of competence and accomplishment while increasing personal growth. At the same time, when you focus on your own personal inventory it allows you to be open to thinking, feeling, or behaving differently if you conclude that what you're doing is not working well in your life. In the long run you can accomplish so much more when you take the focus off of others and redirect it back on yourself.

Keep in mind that the more you attempt to change someone or something else the less energy you have left over for yourself. And again, no matter how much you try you will not change anyone else, nor can you ultimately control what others say or do. You always have the right to decide that someone's behavior or a current life circumstance is unacceptable to you. But once you've made that decision focus your efforts and energy on what *you* can do differently.

Once you've assessed that something in your life upsets you, disappoints or angers you, or leaves you feeling unsafe, it's important to start thinking about what *you* need to do to comfort or protect yourself. This might include changing a boundary, walking away, or finding and creating relationships and situations that can meet your needs and feel good for you. Those are the things you *can* change, so be fierce about putting your efforts there and let go of the rest!

Questions For Continued Growth

— * —

1. Who are the people/what are the situations in your life you spend the most amount of time attempting to fix or change?

_____

_____

_____

_____

_____

_____

_____

_____

2. How do you typically go about trying to fix or change those people or situations?

_____

_____

_____

_____

_____

_____

_____

3. What do you imagine would happen if they didn't change?

_____

_____

_____

_____

_____

_____

_____

_____

_____

4. If you could let go of the energy you expend trying to change a situation or someone else, where would you be channeling that energy instead?

_____

_____

_____

_____

_____

_____

_____

_____

_____

5. What would shift or change in your life once your energy was redirected?

_____

_____

_____

_____

_____

_____

_____

_____

_____

6. What are the positive messages you could give yourself to help you let go of trying to change other people or situations?

_____

_____

_____

_____

_____

_____

_____

_____

Act As If and It Will Become a Reality

This is a very powerful idea and I want to caution you that it can play out in potentially positive or negative ways. First, let's look at the upside to this strategy. Oftentimes people think that behaviors can't be realized, goals reached, or emotions fully experienced unless they wholeheartedly believe in them first. This is actually not the case. Acting "as if" carries tremendous weight, and that's good to know as people often need a way to "jump-start" a new behavior or connection to an unfamiliar feeling.

You might initially reject the idea of acting "as if," claiming that it's dishonest and it feels like you're "faking it." But if you're like most people, the only "as if" behaviors that you'll even attempt to try are the ones you have some interest in mastering. Even the smallest desire or curiosity to accomplish that action or express a buried or important emotion means it's not insincere. You either don't know how to proceed or have trouble trusting that it's possible for you to get there. In those cases, acting "as if" is a great first step.

For example, if you act "as if" you have courage you will eventually uncover that quality in yourself. You can act "as if" by first thinking about courageous people in your life who have displayed those characteristics and then trying them on and acting out those same qualities. When you do this you'll begin to put forth a courageous demeanor and you'll be accessing the courageous part of yourself in the process. Soon the people around you will experience you as courageous. Their feedback becomes another source of reinforcement and begins to shape both their story about you as well as your story about yourself.

When you act "as if" the future is bright you will gravitate towards behavioral choices, thoughts, and feelings that begin to make that prediction true. In fact, acting "as if" any positive and life-affirming message is your reality, in time, *makes* it your reality. This is because so much of what you think consciously and unconsciously influences what you say and do, the people you do and don't interact with, and the environments you do and don't seek out.

As previously mentioned, there is a downside to this life philosophy and it often plays out with people who have histories of trauma, abuse, or neglect. If this is a part of your background it adds to your vulnerability because those painful life experiences tend to create strong feelings of self-blame and shame. If you act "as if" you are damaged, bad, or unworthy you'll make choices related to relationships, your career and workplace environment, parenting, and your medical and mental health, as well as decisions about self-care, that are all in keeping with the idea of being unworthy.

You can see that choices flowing from a core belief of being unworthy can only lead to detrimental or even abusive outcomes. This in turn creates a self-fulfilling prophecy of feeling damaged and bad, which fuels, reinforces, and strengthens that distorted sense of self. And the saddest part of this dynamic is the fact that, objectively speaking, you aren't damaged or bad. Subjectively you've been living "as if" you are and have turned that into your reality. Therein lies the power behind "as if" thinking and behaving.

Take a moment to acknowledge your own "as if" thoughts and behaviors. How many of them are rooted in positive, hope-based notions versus negative, shame-based ones that probably have their origins in unresolved trauma or the inaccurate messages you got from unkind people in your life? Can you identify one small, positive "as if" attribute or goal that you can begin to put into practice? Can you begin to let go of one "as if" thought or behavior that keeps alive a negative sense of self? That would be a giant step forward towards improving your well-being. If you're a parent this is also a great exercise to teach your kids. Acting "as if" they have confidence, can succeed in school, deserve safe and loving friends, and don't need to get drunk in order to fit in can go a long way towards turning those beliefs into reality.

The same is true in your workplace and your personal relationships. Act "as if" you deserve to be treated with respect and kindness, appreciated for your contributions, validated for your thoughts and feelings, and you're more likely to experience those things. And if that isn't the case, act "as if" you're giving yourself permission to change jobs or leave an unfulfilling relationship and that might be exactly what comes to pass!

Questions For Continued Growth

———— * ————

1. Identify one way in which "as if" thinking has negatively impacted your sense of self.

_____

_____

_____

_____

_____

_____

_____

2. Identify one negative "as if" statement that you're interested in letting go of now.

_____

_____

_____

_____

_____

_____

_____

_____

3. What might be the positive impact that "as if" thinking could have on your life?

_____

_____

_____

_____

_____

_____

_____

_____

4. Identify three positive "as if" statements you can make about yourself.

_____

_____

_____

_____

_____

_____

_____

_____

5. Identify two desired behaviors that "as if" thinking could jump start for you.

_____

_____

_____

_____

_____

_____

_____

_____

6. Describe any hesitation you have about using "as if" as a motivational tool in your life. How can you overcome that hesitation?

_____

_____

_____

_____

_____

_____

_____

_____

Change Rarely Happens When You're Comfortable

This life lesson can be initially difficult to understand and accept. Most people work fairly hard to *avoid* feeling discomfort in their lives! Like everyone else you're probably a creature of habit and enjoy the predictability and consistency of doing "what you know." It's not easy to go outside of a well-established "comfort zone." At times when life becomes unpredictable your initial reactions may include fear, anxiety, anger, sadness, helplessness, or a state of being overwhelmed. It's certainly understandable if you can't immediately access a sense of excitement and enthusiasm about something in your world suddenly being turned upside down!

Yet it's genuinely true that the best opportunities you'll ever have for deep, meaningful growth typically occur within a context of discomfort and unpredictability. When you live within the "status quo" it's certainly easier. Without realizing it you can almost approach life in an "automatic pilot" kind of way. Staying within the boundaries of what's familiar doesn't require a lot of thought or effort. On the surface it might seem like the best course of action and the preferred way to live your life.

It's important to acknowledge that there may be periods of time in your life when "coasting" feels necessary, and if that becomes a way to engage in self-care, regroup, or reduce stress, then allow for it. However, "coasting" forever doesn't lead to growth or change.

Take a moment and think about the times in your life when you experienced the greatest amount of change or attempted new behavior that you had not considered trying in the past. Now think about what was going on in your life when you made those changes. Were they times that were predictable and "business as usual" in your work, health, or relationships? In all likelihood something unforeseen was happening and it either gave you a small push or a huge shove that almost forced your hand, propelling you into unchartered terrain.

Is it fair to say that if the crisis or profound shift didn't happen in your life you probably wouldn't have made the changes or experienced the personal or professional growth that you did? For most people this is the case. As a therapist I witness people enter into the process of therapy because they're faced with a crisis or something unexpected that has occurred in their lives. Obviously they don't start therapy when everything is going smoothly!

Of course it's natural to initially be quite shaken when the rug is pulled out from under you. It's hard to focus on the potential, down- the-road positive outcomes when you're in an immediate state of discomfort. But time and time again I have watched people grow in remarkable ways because they're in a state of "being off balance" and are forced to re-evaluate important aspects of their lives.

During the course of therapy and the journey of working through something traumatic, this re-evaluation can lead to significant changes, and that's where the growth happens. Priorities shift, important new decisions are made, deeper feelings are accessed and processed, and old habits are replaced with healthier behaviors.

Try to embrace the notion that being thrown a curve ball can create opportunities for you to connect with newfound inner strengths and resiliency, creativity, previously untapped insights and resources. It's often a crisis that leads to releasing yourself from a toxic or unfulfilling job. A profound tipping point in a relationship creates the opportunity to re-evaluate whether or not you're really getting your needs met.

This life lesson plays out on a communal and societal level as well. The tragedy of a terrorist attack, natural disaster, or violent crime often becomes the catalyst for meaningful changes in social policy, national security, or a re-examination of the environment. Doesn't it seem like communities and even our government can remain disinterested and emotionally unmoved until deeply disturbing events such as these unfold and are suddenly talked about on a national level?

That's not to say that we wish traumatic experiences on anyone in order for growth to occur! But the reality is experiences in life can sometimes be traumatic or overwhelming. So if an unsolicited challenge enters your life, know that this mindset can prepare you and enable you to face it with less fear and anxiety. In time you might even be able to reframe it as an opportunity or the experience that jump-started lasting and meaningful growth and change.

Questions For Continued Growth

——— * ———

1. Describe a time in your life when you were thrown an
   unexpected curve ball.

   _____

   _____

   _____

   _____

   _____

   _____

   _____

   _____

2. What were your initial reactions and the initial by-products of
   that unplanned event?

   _____

   _____

   _____

   _____

   _____

   _____

   _____

3. What internal and external resources did you call upon to get through the crisis?

_____

_____

_____

_____

_____

_____

_____

_____

_____

4. In what ways did you personally or professionally grow as a result of that crisis?

_____

_____

_____

_____

_____

_____

_____

_____

5. What would have remained the same if that difficult experience had not occurred?

_____

_____

_____

_____

_____

_____

_____

_____

_____

6. How have your priorities changed as a result of that experience?

_____

_____

_____

_____

_____

_____

_____

_____

_____

Wake-Up Loving Yourself and Notice What's Different in Your Life

One of the subtle but powerful aspects of life is the extent to which your thoughts, feelings, and behaviors are influenced and impacted by self-love versus self-loathing. Even if you're not consciously aware of this you gravitate towards certain choices and ignore or dismiss other options based upon how you honestly feel about yourself. It's a valuable exercise to consider what would change in your relationships, healthy risk taking, career choices, acts of self-care, contributions to your community, and even the environment where you choose to live if all of those decisions were guided by a core feeling of loving yourself.

So allow yourself to imagine that upon awakening one day you looked in the mirror and genuinely loved what you saw. Not in an arrogant or boastful way. Just in a way that produced a calm feeling of self-acceptance and self-worth. Perhaps the way you feel towards a beloved pet or when you enjoy the warm and loving company of a friend or family member.

If you could generate those feelings of love and acceptance for yourself how would it impact your choices? Perhaps it would be easier to set limits and healthy boundaries in your interactions with others so you could feel safe. It might be more natural to say "No" when you genuinely wanted to say 'No" to avoid being overly stressed, burdened, or overwhelmed.

You might find it easier to say "Yes" to the healthy risks, adventures, and out-of-the-box experiences that would enrich your life but which have historically created feelings of fear or anxiety. If you loved yourself more it would increase your self-confidence and strengthen a belief that you could tackle new challenges with competence. You'd feel worthy of new experiences and see unfamiliar terrain as an opportunity for growth rather than an obstacle to be avoided.

If you woke up loving yourself the choices you made about healthier eating habits, making sure to exercise, and being committed to getting adequate sleep might feel natural and easier to achieve. If you became ill the idea of seeing a doctor and getting your symptoms checked out and addressed would be second nature. You would understand the importance of being compliant in taking medication and making whatever lifestyle choices were necessary to improve your physical and mental well-being.

Seeking psychological support for stress or unresolved trauma would feel like the right thing to do. Your ambivalence would be replaced with a clear understanding that you have the right to be supported in your healing process. Going it alone would no longer make sense to you. You might become very protective of your medical and mental health needs, making sure that the daily obligations of life never trumped your right to good health.

You might re-evaluate your current job situation and probably have a much lower tolerance for dysfunctional workplace dynamics, inadequate pay, or an unsupportive boss or colleagues who took your hard work for granted and never expressed appreciation for your efforts and accomplishments.

If you woke up loving yourself and, therefore, felt worthy of being loved, you might take a closer look at your intimate relationships. Your threshold for being treated poorly or co-existing in an unfulfilling partnership would be significantly lowered. You would insist upon being treated with kindness and respect. You would be able to communicate your needs and your feelings effectively and without shame. You could accept and embrace compliments and return them in kind without questioning anyone's "ulterior motive."

In all likelihood you would experience a significant reduction in negative self-talk and you'd come to believe that motivating yourself through humiliation or shame was ineffective and unfair. The voice of inner criticism or perfectionism that at times held you hostage and never allowed you to feel "good enough" would disappear. If you operated from a stronger sense of self-love and self-worth your ability to access inner wisdom and self-compassion would dramatically increase. Even when you took a misstep or made a mistake you could learn from it and grow rather than beating yourself up about it.

So allow yourself to consider the possibility that you can increase self-love and self-acceptance. Tell yourself it's within your reach. Make it an actual intention; when you go to sleep tonight and wake up in the morning you'll be a step closer to the inner peace that comes with genuinely caring about yourself and your well-being.

Questions For Continued Growth

—— * ——

1. When you consider the possibility of being able to love yourself more what do you think and feel?

_____

_____

_____

_____

_____

_____

_____

_____

2. Identify an experience that may have prevented you from greater self-love.

_____

_____

_____

_____

_____

_____

_____

3. How can you either re-think that experience or let it go so it no longer prevents you from loving yourself?

_____

_____

_____

_____

_____

_____

_____

_____

4. If you woke up tomorrow loving yourself more what would be different in your relationships?

_____

_____

_____

_____

_____

_____

_____

_____

5. If you woke up tomorrow loving yourself more what would change in your professional life?

_____

_____

_____

_____

_____

_____

_____

_____

_____

6. If you woke up tomorrow loving yourself more what would change in terms of your self-care?

_____

_____

_____

_____

_____

_____

_____

_____

_____

Be Afraid,
Do It Anyway

You have a wonderful imagination! It allows you to dream big dreams. You can think about experiences that haven't even happened yet and those thoughts can motivate you to become a healthy risk-taker, turning your daydreams into reality. Your imagination offers you a chance to tap into deep levels of creativity, to suspend disbelief and allow for wonder, or activate a sense of hope for the future. But in addition to the uplifting ways in which you use your imagination your thoughts also have the power to generate fear and anxiety.

It's possible that one of the biggest reasons why you hesitate or don't take chances that would allow you to grow and enrich your life is because you're afraid. Being afraid is a normal and healthy response to the unknown. However, if you're like most people you have convinced yourself that being afraid means, by definition, that you can't move ahead. In fact, whether you realize it or not you might feel forced to maintain the status quo until you're no longer afraid. See if this thought sounds familiar: "First I have to get rid of my fear *and then* I can take steps towards accomplishing my goals or trying a new behavior."

The problem and the irony is you will probably continue to be afraid as long as you don't make a move! In this stalled state you continue to imagine the worst, with no actual positive experiences to challenge your point of reference or challenge your fears. In essence you're being held hostage by fear and this leaves you in a paralyzed state.

What often fuels fear is the "unknown." But if you stay frozen and never venture into that arena you keep it unknown and actually increase your fear and anxiety about it. Taking steps to make the unknown familiar is one important way to reduce your fears.

Now tap into your imagination and think about what could happen if you took the power away from fear by allowing it to exist *and* not allowing it to stop you from moving ahead. Fear and taking action doesn't have to be a mutually exclusive proposition. What you can do is acknowledge that you feel fear, understand it, and really let yourself experience it. As you do that, you can reach out for support if it's helpful. Take the time to soothe and comfort your sense of fear, rather than ignoring it. That is often the first step in *working with* your fears. And while you do those things you can still begin to move forward, trusting your ability to navigate fear as you meet the challenges and the excitement of your goals and your dreams head on. In other words, break the connection between "I'm afraid" and "Therefore, I can't."

When you don't allow fear to stop you it begins to lose its power. It's just another emotion. You can consciously decide if there's valuable guidance and meaning in it. Sometimes fear lets you know that the situation or a personal interaction is truly unsafe and you need to respond accordingly. In those instances being afraid is a good source of protection and should be factored into your decision making process. Maybe it's telling you to "proceed with caution," make a firmer plan, get outside feedback, or put other things in place before moving ahead.

But much of the time it's just an emotion that's rooted in your past experiences and may not be relevant at all to your current abilities and life situation. In those instances be afraid and do it anyway. You will discover that the fear begins to lessen as soon as you take that first proactive and empowering step. Otherwise, you may be 90-years-old and still waiting in a holding pattern for the fear to subside!

Questions For Continued Growth

———— * ————

1. When you feel afraid how does that manifest in your thoughts and on your body?

_____

_____

_____

_____

_____

_____

_____

_____

_____

2. What is something you've always wanted to do but haven't done yet because you've been held back by fear?

_____

_____

_____

_____

_____

_____

_____

_____

3. What would shift or change in your life if you accomplished what you identified in the above question?

_____

_____

_____

_____

_____

_____

_____

_____

4. Identify a time when you were afraid and still realized your goals.

_____

_____

_____

_____

_____

_____

_____

_____

_____

_____

5. What enabled you to succeed despite your fears?

_____

_____

_____

_____

_____

_____

_____

_____

_____

6. How can you replicate that in your life now?

_____

_____

_____

_____

_____

_____

_____

_____

_____

* * * * *

PART 5

Self-Compassion

Throughout this book you've been given many opportunities to learn about how the relationships and experiences you had growing up impacted the messages you carry inside of yourself about yourself. It's possible that you've made important new connections and now have a deeper understanding of prior choices and the thoughts that have guided them.

This section of the book reinforces those connections and in doing so is designed to keep moving you away from self-blame or shame. Understanding that poor decisions or personal struggles make sense "given where you come from" is a very freeing concept and can help you let go of the false belief that there's "something wrong with you." This strengthens self-compassion: one of the best antidotes to shame.

As you continue to incorporate the little life lessons that can add up to big changes another important concept to hold on to is the fact that so much of your life is now in your power and control! You get to attach meaning to experiences and that can either keep you angry and stuck or move you forward. You have the power to focus on the things you do right rather than the things you've done wrong or regret. It's in your power to embrace *all* of who you are rather than trying to disown the parts that make you uncomfortable or embarrassed.

The key concept of self-compassion allows you to take everything you've discovered about yourself and look at it with loving eyes. There is no better motivator than kind words and the core belief that you're loveable and worthy of a truly satisfying life.

It Makes Sense Given Where You've Come From

When you struggle with certain issues or symptoms it's human nature and logical to want to know "why?" Having an explanation for the repeated pattern of self-defeating choices, a constant sense of unhappiness or pessimism, an inability to trust or feel close to people, a compulsion to hurt your body through self-destructive behaviors, or anything else you grapple with, somehow makes that feeling or behavior more understandable or acceptable. Explanations allow you to rationalize or justify your behavior.

However, if you're like most people the explanations you've come up with focus around a central, powerful, and unfounded idea: You do dysfunctional things or struggle with overwhelming feelings because there's something fundamentally wrong with you. As painful as it is to go through life with the inner belief that you're "damaged," "broken," "bad," or "crazy," at least it's a way to make sense out of issues that confuse or embarrass you.

One of the most important and freeing life lessons you can consider is the idea that who you are, what you feel, and what you do all make sense given where you've come from. "Where you've come from" has everything to do with the experiences you had in your family growing up. This includes the physical, financial, spiritual, and emotional environment you were raised in, the messages you were taught about yourself and the world, and how others treated you. There are also countless other factors that make up your personal narrative and autobiography as you travel through life and interact with other people.

Where you've come from serves as a compass, roadmap, and silent guide for many of your later experiences and choices. Your relationships reflect your sense of yourself and what you've been taught you do and don't deserve to receive from others. The extent to which you engage in self-harm or self-care connects to how your caretakers treated your body. Being able to use your voice to advocate for your rights or feeling forced to stay silent has its roots in your past. The parenting tools that were or were not put in your toolbox impact your ability to appropriately, effectively, and lovingly parent your own children.

As you read this it might seem obvious that those factors would profoundly influence anyone's life as well as their sense of self-esteem and many of their future choices. And yet it's still quite likely that when it comes to your own life and behaviors you have significantly minimized or even completely ignored the impact those experiences have had on you. Instead you may have spent a lifetime telling yourself the reason why you behave in ways that are "different," "inferior," or "weird" is because you're somehow defective.

As a therapist I can tell you that when someone who struggles begins to "connect the dots" and realizes that who they are, how they think and feel, and what they do has everything to do with where they've come from, they're put on the path towards true healing. It's the first step away from self-blame and shame. And that creates the possibility to let in self-compassion and self-forgiveness.

Although building this bridge between all of your past experiences and your current "symptoms" is a powerful way to let go of self-blame, it doesn't mean you aren't responsible for changing your behavior and making different choices in the future. The life lesson is that you're not responsible for what was done to you in the past and you are totally responsible for what you do with it now.

The value of accepting the idea that it all "makes sense given where you've come from" is that it sets you free from the belief that you're crazy or incapable of change. However, it's worth noting that when you genuinely consider the impact of the experiences you had growing up it may bring up difficult emotions for you. This can include facing the painful reality that other people profoundly and negatively affected your life. That truth can create legitimate feelings of anger, sadness, betrayal, loss, and helplessness.

It might also stir up confusion as it's always challenging, and even scary, to say negative things about one's parents or upbringing. You might initially feel disloyal or worried that it will change your current relationship with family members. Acknowledging painful facts from the past can unlock deeply buried feelings and memories that resurface without your wanting them to, intensifying your emotional upset or even triggering more destructive behaviors in the short-term as you attempt to numb the pain.

This is why it's frequently necessary to explore the reality of your past with a compassionate, trained professional who can help pace the work and provide you with additional resources for comfort and support. As challenging as it might sound to connect your issues to childhood and other influential experiences and relationships, in the long run it frees you up to see yourself in a whole new and much more loving light.

Questions For Continued Growth

———— * ————

1. Historically, how have you made sense out of the things you've struggled with in life?

_____

_____

_____

_____

_____

_____

_____

_____

_____

2. What do you imagine would happen if you accepted the notion that your struggles made sense "given where you've come from?

_____

_____

_____

_____

_____

_____

_____

_____

3. What would you gain if you adopted this new mindset?

_____

_____

_____

_____

_____

_____

_____

_____

4. What would you lose if you adopted this new mindset?

_____

_____

_____

_____

_____

_____

_____

_____

_____

5. Identify one symptom you've struggled with and connect it to a family of origin experience.

_____

_____

_____

_____

_____

_____

_____

_____

_____

6. What shift or changes occurs for you when you give yourself permission to do that?

_____

_____

_____

_____

_____

_____

_____

_____

There's Nothing More Powerful than the Way You Talk to Yourself about Yourself

If you're like a lot of people you probably wonder or worry about what others think of or say about you. Many people expend tremendous energy on this and often work hard to modify or change their actions in an attempt to make sure that friends, co-workers, bosses, family members, spouses, kids, or even strangers don't think poorly of them. The ironic truth is no matter what anyone else thinks or says about you, there's nothing more powerful than the messages you give to yourself about yourself.

This is such an important life lesson because your own inner monologue profoundly influences you. It guides the extent to which you do or don't criticize yourself, or feel empathy and compassion for your mistakes and allow yourself to learn from them. The way you talk to yourself and the messages you repeat impact whether or not you go out of your comfort zone, take healthy risks, and expand your life experiences. In fact, most of your thoughts, emotions, and behaviors flow from those internal messages. They affect your ability to be self-protective, create and sustain intimate relationships, challenge yourself to personally grow or try novel things, be a nurturing and available parent, trust your own instincts, and have the confidence and self-esteem that is needed to succeed in life.

Once you realize that the voice in your own head ultimately shapes your moods and actions you can begin to take the focus off of what other people say. This can free you up a lot. Part of why you might be trying to please other people or give too much weight to what others think is because you've falsely believed that their approval or input was the ultimate source of your own self-worth.

The voice that is strongest in your head is your own. And yet it's important to realize that some of the messages you hear might have been given to you by other people, and aren't your own authentic ideas. This is especially true when you were young. Your parents and other caretakers gave you all kinds of messages about who you were and how you should feel about yourself. This creates a kind of tape recording in your mind that can play over and over again.

The tricky thing is, you never initially questioned those messages that played on your tape and drowned out your own thoughts. Like everyone else you trusted the feedback you got from people who were highly credible because they were parental or authority figures and supposedly had your best interests at heart. So you might have accepted messages that shamed you and compromised your confidence and self-esteem, not realizing the long-term impact it would have, and certainly not challenging the legitimacy of those ideas.

But the good news is when you reach a certain age you can begin to re-evaluate those messages and decide which ones are helpful or objectively true. You get to decide the kind of content you want playing on your inner tape. And once you do that your own voice becomes the single greatest guide in all of your future choices.

Part of why this is so important to accept is that the only thing you really have control over and can impact and change is your own voice. Rather than spinning your wheels trying to get other people to think well of you, redirect your efforts and energy and begin to explore the ways in which you can improve your own inner monologue.

Do your thoughts help motivate you to grow and move forward in life or do they hold you back? Are you your own best cheerleader or does that monologue leave you feeling embarrassed, ashamed, or unworthy? Do you focus on your strengths and the meaningful contributions you have made, or dwell on what you believe to be your weaknesses or "failures?"

In addition to noticing the content of your inner messages, pay as much attention to the tone. The *way* you speak to yourself is just as important as what you say. Are the messages delivered in a voice that is sarcastic or bullying? Do you sometimes yell at yourself in your head? Is your running monologue laced with anger or put-downs? There's a false belief in our culture that berating, harsh words can somehow have the effect of motivating you to grow and change. The opposite is true. When you talk to yourself in ways that are shaming and humiliating you are *less* likely to accomplish anything productive. Harsh words hold you back in life, especially when they come from your own inner voice.

One way to check on that inner monologue is to take some time to notice what you think, feel, and say when you look at your own reflection in the mirror. Know that those are the experiences that ultimately define who you are and what you believe you can and cannot accomplish. And if you recognize that the messages are not supportive or loving, find the courage to take the first baby step towards experimenting with gently challenging them and changing your tone of voice.

Ask yourself, "Is it possible this message I got about myself was wrong?" "Is there a different, kinder way I can talk to myself about a particular issue?" When you begin to allow yourself to re-evaluate the messages you've always blindly accepted as "truths," while also softening your tone of voice, it becomes easier to let go of destructive thoughts and open up to the possibility of embracing more loving ones.

Questions For Continued Growth

———— * ————

1. List three of the most common messages you tell yourself throughout the day.

   _____

   _____

   _____

   _____

   _____

   _____

   _____

   _____

   _____

2. When you think about those messages what is the "tone of voice" that accompanies them?

   _____

   _____

   _____

   _____

   _____

   _____

   _____

   _____

3. Describe a time when you were able to talk to yourself in a compassionate and kind way.

_____

_____

_____

_____

_____

_____

_____

_____

4. What made it possible to do that?

_____

_____

_____

_____

_____

_____

_____

_____

_____

5. Who are the people in your life who could model talking to yourself in a kinder way?

_____

_____

_____

_____

_____

_____

_____

_____

6. Identify the words and tone you would use to motivate someone you cared deeply about.

_____

_____

_____

_____

_____

_____

_____

_____

What Matters Most Is the Meaning You Attach to Experiences

Many things have happened throughout your life. Some of those situations have felt "wonderful" and others have felt "terrible." Like most people you probably believe that life events and personal interactions are either "good" or "bad" and then respond to them accordingly. You might feel delighted, lucky, or grateful when "good" things happen, and angry, scared, cheated, or victimized when "bad" things occur.

But what if these events and experiences were mostly "neutral?" What if the way in which you reacted to them was rooted more in the *meaning* that you consciously or unconsciously attached to them rather than the experiences themselves? I realize this can initially feel like a radical idea. Surely there must be some life events that by everyone's standards are just plain "bad" or "tragic" or "wonderful."

And yet as a therapist I've witnessed people reacting in ways that seem to directly contradict how the world would think about and label certain experiences. It's not uncommon for 10 people to witness or participate in the exact same experience and react in 10 different ways. It has made me realize that it's not really about the event itself: it's the meaning you attach to the event that influences the specific ways in which you think, feel, and respond to what has taken place.

Believe it or not this can be good news! This mindset allows you to focus on what you *can* control about the situation and helps dictate the ways in which life events do and don't affect you. It's empowering to know that you have the ability to look at an experience through more than one lens. You get to decide whether or not the situation has defeated you or strengthened you. You decide whether or not to take it personally.

There are people who see a sunny day and "wait for the other shoe to drop," choosing to believe that rain clouds are probably right around the corner. As a result they stay inside, depriving themselves of sunshine while waiting for the rain to come. And when the rain does come, they experience it as further "proof" that all things eventually get ruined.

Others see the sunshine through a positive lens and don't even think about the possibility of rain. They choose to savor the warm outdoors and if the clouds do roll in and the raindrops fall they choose to see that as a great opportunity for the flowers to be watered! Same event, yet attaching completely different meanings yields very different emotions and behavioral choices.

Obviously sunshine and rain clouds are a simplistic example. But I've seen people attach meaning to deeply traumatic and upsetting events in ways that either paralyze and defeat them or enable them to tap into remarkable resiliency and thrive.

Think about this life lesson of "meaning making" and notice the ways in which you respond to both small and deeply impactful experiences. Ask yourself if anything could shift or change for you if you chose to attach a *different* meaning to those same experiences. Since you can never undo and often cannot control what has already occurred your power lives in your ability to find meaning that will move you forward, promote self-compassion, and help you to heal.

The longer you live the clearer it becomes that "stuff happens." The real question and life lesson is, "Now what do you want to do about it?" Know that the meaning you attach to an event will often guide, in subtle and profound ways, what you "do with it" in the short and long term. Having a more conscious awareness about your responses to powerful life events is the key to determining the path that you'll follow.

When the meaning supports ideas such as the world is out to get you, people can't be trusted, you'll never succeed, everyone is selfish, you'll always be alone, or you're unlovable, that often leads to a path of re-victimization and intense feelings of helplessness and hopelessness. This in turn creates a shutting down of emotions, isolation and a refusal to reconnect with others, heightened defensiveness, chronic bitterness, and an unwillingness to take risks.

However, there's a different mindset that you can attach to traumatic events. Changing the meaning can begin to move you in a very different direction. Trauma can inspire a belief that there's a lesson to learn, confirm the humble reality that some things are not in your control, and promote the idea that when a bad thing happens it doesn't mean *you* are bad. These thoughts will then lead to a significant change in behaviors. Social connection, a focus on resiliency, opportunities to act creatively, a move toward forgiveness, and the desire to pay it forward all forge a path that can lead to remarkable growth and positive changes in your life.

Questions For Continued Growth

*

1. When challenging things happen in your life what meaning do you usually attach to those events?

_____

_____

_____

_____

_____

_____

_____

2. Who taught you to look at life events through that lens?

_____

_____

_____

_____

_____

_____

_____

3. How does that meaning impact you emotionally, physically, and behaviorally?

_____

_____

_____

_____

_____

_____

_____

_____

4. When challenging things happen in your life what meaning do the significant people in your life attach to those events?

_____

_____

_____

_____

_____

_____

_____

_____

5. Identify a time when something difficult or challenging happened and the meaning you attached strengthened you.

_____

_____

_____

_____

_____

_____

_____

_____

6. What internal and external resources did you draw upon to attach meaning that strengthened rather than defeated you?

_____

_____

_____

_____

_____

_____

_____

_____

Celebrate Your Successes—Stop Obsessing about Your Failures

Think about the amount of energy you spend focusing on your past mistakes, regretting your behavioral choices, or beating yourself up for the way you emotionally responded to a challenging situation or person. Now imagine if you channeled that same amount of energy into noticing, cataloging, and acknowledging the small and large things you've done and continue to do that are positive and successful. If you're like a lot of people there's probably an imbalance in what you do and don't focus on.

Why should your mistakes get so much more attention than your successes? This can only leave you with a skewed and distorted sense of self. If the great stuff you do gets ignored and the normal ways in which you fall short get highlighted, and probably exaggerated, what story will you wind up telling yourself about who you are? And how will that story influence your present and future choices?

If it still feels more natural for you to shine a spotlight on the "failures" it's certainly worth becoming curious about why you feel drawn to focus more on your mistakes and shortcomings and why it feels so challenging or counter-intuitive to pay attention to the times when you succeed. Sometime it's just as important to know *why* you make the choices you do as it is to move in the direction of changing those choices.

For many people their earliest relationships with important people in their lives served as the role model for how to think about themselves. In other words you were taught in childhood and throughout your growing up years which behaviors were important to focus on because those were the ones your parents, teachers, siblings, and peers focused on. Important people in your life held up "mirrors" to you, influencing the reflection that you saw. In reality, you saw yourself through *their* eyes, not your own.

In addition to noticing certain behaviors and ignoring others you were also taught how to think about them and how to attach meaning to them. Labels of "good," "bad," "acceptable," "inappropriate," "successful," and "failure" were given to you by people you loved and trusted. In time you began to make these assessments automatically, never stopping to challenge the labels. If your parents categorized and judged your missteps as "failures" rather than using your mistakes as opportunities to help you learn and grow, it would be easy for you to continue this negative labeling and mindset throughout your adult life.

It could be that your parents, teachers, and the other influential adults in your life downplayed or even ignored your accomplishments, either because they were threatened by your successes or set the bar so high that *nothing* ever met their criteria for success. If this is the case it might explain why it's so difficult for you to acknowledge those achievements or have trouble trusting or believing other people when they enthusiastically point them out.

At the very least, allow yourself to be more accurate and fair in the ways that you judge your day-to-day behaviors. If it feels necessary to keep acknowledging when you do something wrong, isn't it only reasonable to also commit to catching yourself doing things right? This more balanced approach helps to soften the upset feelings when you do inevitably make a mistake—which you will, because you're human!

This idea of "catching yourself" doing something right might take a fair amount of practice. After all, you've been conditioned to automatically shine the spotlight on the "failures," which keeps your accomplishments in the dark. Don't give up if you start to notice how often you focus on the ways in which you fall short. Once this is called to your attention you might be surprised by how frequently you do it. You'll also discover how much work it initially takes to re-think situations and your actions in an attempt to notice the positives. As you begin identifying the small and larger successes you might discover that they were hiding in the wings all the time. The more you practice shining a light on your accomplishments, retraining your brain to notice and acknowledge them, the easier it gets.

It often helps to consider whether the yardstick you use to measure "successes" and "failures" in loved ones is the same standard you use when labeling those behaviors in yourself. It's quite likely that the bar is much lower when you feel moved to compliment someone else or feel comfortable defining what others have done as a success worthy of acknowledgment.

On the other hand, a whole lot of missteps might have to unfold before you're willing to weigh in and label someone else's behavior as a "failure." You're operating from a double standard when you jump in sooner to compliment what others have done and hold back a lot longer before judging their actions as failures. What would it be like if you applied that same standard to your own behaviors? In all likelihood you would compliment yourself more often and beat yourself up a whole lot less. And as we have previously discussed, beating yourself up will never effectively motivate you to achieve more. Quite the opposite; the shame and humiliation you create is far more likely to hold you back.

Questions For Continued Growth

———— * ————

1. While you were growing up did the significant people in your life emphasize your mistakes or your accomplishments?

_____

_____

_____

_____

_____

_____

_____

_____

2. What impact did it have when they focused on your mistakes rather than your successes?

_____

_____

_____

_____

_____

_____

3. What do you imagine would happen if you focused less on your mistakes and chose to focus on your successes?

_____

_____

_____

_____

_____

_____

_____

_____

4. Shine a spotlight on three successes you have had in your life.

_____

_____

_____

_____

_____

_____

_____

_____

_____

5. What do you notice you think and feel when you allow yourself to focus on your successes?

_____

_____

_____

_____

_____

_____

_____

_____

6. What would it take for you to do that more often?

_____

_____

_____

_____

_____

_____

_____

_____

You Can't Cut Off Your Left Arm and Still be Whole

How often have you thought to yourself, "If I could just get rid of the part of me that I can't stand—the habit, personality, physical trait, emotion, thought, behavior or experience from the past—then I'd be just fine?" You may relate to the idea that there's something or perhaps many things about yourself that hold you back, preventing you from really being okay. If you operate from this mindset you'll understand that the natural tendency is to think about how to "get rid of" whatever shames you or what you don't like about yourself.

Sometimes this is a conscious process that might include keeping that part of yourself hidden from other people, ignoring what you don't like and pretending it doesn't exist, overcompensating for it, or actively looking for ways to give it up. Whatever you're doing, know that it consumes a lot of energy and the irony is it won't bring you any closer to feeling good about yourself. This is because trying to get rid of any aspect of yourself is like attempting to cut off your left arm and then imagining that without it you can be whole.

There are so many things that make you who you are, including your past experiences and all of the qualities and

187

characteristics that are both internally wired, modeled, and reinforced by other people. You're profoundly influenced by your genetic make-up and temperament, relationships, environment, culture, spiritual and religious experiences, and beliefs. The key to really feeling okay is to start by *accepting* who you are with self-compassion rather than harsh judgment or criticism. If there are things symbolically represented by your "left arm" that make you unhappy, insecure, or ashamed, start by acknowledging that reality and then look at how you can begin to compassionately address those things. But recognize that you can't simply cut off that left arm!

Sometimes this means working to reach a place of acceptance. This is particularly important when you're dealing with experiences from the past that have already occurred and cannot be undone or changed. Rather than continually fighting them or pretending they don't exist, consider the life lesson of working towards a calm acceptance of them. Or focus on the fact that you endured and survived them and try to find a sense of pride and peace in that.

Maybe the thing you're trying to get rid of from your past or within yourself has something to teach you. Think about the possibility that you can learn from and grow from your "left arm" rather than trying to continually disown it. When you do that you're decreasing internal tension and allowing yourself to move forward toward inner peace.

There may be aspects of your personality or your physical appearance that trouble you. It's reasonable to ask if there are concrete, productive things you can do to work on self-improvement. But ironically, even in those cases, the place to start is to stop fighting yourself and recognize that these qualities may either be what you were born with or are the inevitable by-product of past experiences that were not in your control. If you can learn to embrace rather than fight "what is," you can then move in the direction of changing what is appropriate and in your power to change.

Questions For Continued Growth

———— * ————

1. List three things about yourself that you've always struggled to accept.

   _____

   _____

   _____

   _____

   _____

   _____

   _____

2. Why has it been so difficult to accept those things?

   _____

   _____

   _____

   _____

   _____

   _____

   _____

   _____

3. In the past, how have you responded to or thought about the things you've disliked about yourself?

_____

_____

_____

_____

_____

_____

_____

_____

4. What would shift or change for you if you made the decision to accept and stop judging those things?

_____

_____

_____

_____

_____

_____

_____

_____

5. Identify something you've struggled with about yourself and consider the ways in which you could learn from it instead.

_____

_____

_____

_____

_____

_____

_____

_____

6. Describe what happens when you shift from self-criticism to compassion and acceptance.

_____

_____

_____

_____

_____

_____

_____

_____

You've Been Wearing the Ruby Slippers All Along

Years ago I had the great privilege of working with a young woman who wanted to address her dysfunctional childhood in therapy. Growing up in a home with an alcoholic mother and an emotionally unavailable father left her with the inevitable by-product of low self-esteem. For years she struggled with not feeling good about herself. She believed the only way to feel worthwhile was to please everyone around her. In essence, she thought that "someone out there" had the key to her happiness and if she could figure out a way to win them over she would finally be okay.

After years of coming to terms with and healing her traumatic past she ended therapy and shortly thereafter sent me a beautiful card. The inscription simply said, "Thank you for teaching me that I was wearing the ruby slippers all along." This sentiment has always stayed with me and the wisdom in it is profound.

Think about Dorothy in *The Wizard of Oz* and how she spends the entire movie trying to find her way back home. She is convinced that the wizard holds the answer. In fact, the scarecrow, tin man, and cowardly lion also believe that if they could just reach the Emerald City and get to see the wizard, *he* would provide them with everything they believed they were missing in their lives.

Of course at the end of the movie what they all discover is that everything they yearn for and are trying to find *outside* of themselves already existed *within*. The wizard is nothing more than a small man hiding behind a curtain. He possesses no great magical powers. When Dorothy is instructed to simply "look down at her own feet" she discovers that she's always been wearing the ruby slippers: she's always had everything she needed to find her way back home.

Although it's certainly true that we sometimes need and deserve the support and guidance of other people, it's equally true that there's no greater power than our own inner wisdom. It's important to let go of the idea that your spouse, child, boss, parent, co-worker, or friend is somehow dangling your ruby slippers in front of you or being unkind and hiding them just out of your reach.

That would mean you're giving your power over to them and you can never be happy unless they choose to cooperate and give you back your slippers. And that can translate into spending a lot of energy trying to appease or trick other people in order to get that cooperation. With this mindset you will forever be looking outward for the answers. In actuality they are always found within. The one place you never seem to look.

The card that I received from that young, once-traumatized woman proved she had truly healed because she finally recognized that her ability to feel worthwhile, make good choices, and set boundaries with toxic people in her life was all *internally* driven by her capacity to love, believe in, and protect herself.

You, too, have been wearing the ruby slippers all along. No other person or situation is holding them or keeping them from you. Your ability to feel productive and proud of what you do in your work is not rooted in the evaluation you get from your supervisor. The extent to which you believe you are a loveable and worthwhile partner is not riding on whether or not you get a present for Valentine's Day. Believing in what you have to offer as a parent is not based upon how often your children express their gratitude for your love and concern.

That's not to say that you don't deserve the outstanding evaluation, bouquet of flowers, and verbal praise—you do. It's just that holding your breath and waiting for it, and then feeling unworthy or inadequate when it doesn't come is terribly disempowering, and it shouldn't be the yardstick you use to measure your sense of self.

Write yourself a glowing thank-you note when you know you've done something meaningful. Buy yourself a beautiful bouquet of flowers. Pat yourself on the back when you know you effectively navigated a difficult parenting situation—especially when you handled it in an exhausted state or without much outside support. Take a deep breath and look down. Look at your own feet. That's where you'll find your ruby slippers!

Questions For Continued Growth

—— * ——

1. What powers do your ruby slippers possess?

_____

_____

_____

_____

_____

_____

_____

_____

2. Describe a time when you thought someone else had your ruby slippers. What was that like for you?

_____

_____

_____

_____

_____

_____

_____

_____

3. Describe a time when you realized you were wearing the ruby slippers all along.

_____

_____

_____

_____

_____

_____

_____

_____

4. What are three small gifts you can give yourself to acknowledge your worth?

_____

_____

_____

_____

_____

_____

_____

_____

5. What are three positive statements you can make about yourself to acknowledge your worth?

_____

_____

_____

_____

_____

_____

_____

_____

6. Who are the people in your life who can remind you that the ruby slippers are on your feet?

_____

_____

_____

_____

_____

_____

_____

_____

———— * ————

As you continue to grow and heal remember that everything you need to be and all that you want to be lives inside of you.

Keep accessing your wisdom, strengths, creativity, resiliency, and compassion and know that the sky's the limit.

Now go fly!